Population Processes
in Social Systems

Population Processes in Social Systems

JAMES M. BESHERS

THE FREE PRESS, *New York*
COLLIER-MACMILLAN LIMITED, *London*

Preface

THIS book has grown out of my graduate training, out of my research, and out of my teaching. Many of the leading ideas were formulated while I was a student and both my undergraduate training in history and my graduate training in general have been very useful in this work.

Some remarks on my own experience in teaching the population course might be helpful. Ordinarily I spend six weeks on the material in Chapter 1 and Chapter 2. There is a need for copious illustration and documentation of the international comparisons that I have condensed in the text. At the same time it is well for the student to perform some analysis of these materials himself. Therefore I assign a major outside problem. The student must select two nations, one early in the demographic transition and one late, and analyze the historical demographic and social information that enables him to write a critique of Malthus, of Marx, and of the demographic transition theory itself. The two readers assembled by Spengler and Duncan are an invaluable asset for this phase of the course. The latter part of the course can emphasize either the social psychological issues in Chapters 3, 4, 5, and 6, or the quantitative issues in the Appendix, depending upon the background and interests of the students enrolled. I have usually presented these materials as a liberal arts course with a predominantly undergraduate enrollment, but I have also adapted the course to a specialized graduate student group.

I wish to acknowledge the helpful influence of various persons, in particular among my teachers, Rupert B. Vance, Daniel O. Price, and Reuben Hill, all of whom conceived of population problems and population research in a broad context of social theory, social data, and social measurement techniques. Among many of my own students Eleanor N. Nishiura, Philip Olson, and Lois K. Cohen have made research contributions, especially to Chapter 5.

Preliminary bibliographic work was done by Gerald Solomon. Final bibliographic work, the selection and preparation of tabular and graphic material, and general assembly of the manuscript were performed by James Peters. The draft manuscript was read by Charles Tilly, David Heer, and Frederick Iklé.

JAMES M. BESHERS

Contents

Figures and Tables

Population Processes
in Social Systems

Introduction

THE gathering storm clouds of a world population crisis are now ominously visible to all. What is the nature of this crisis? What can be done to avert it?

If we are to find answers to these questions we must first examine the specialized research literature on the general subject of population and birth control—the main body of knowledge available to a small number of devoted scholars. In summarizing this literature I have striven to remove esoteric and technical obstacles from the path of the reader, in hopes of attracting a broader audience interested in learning more about this truly vital subject. At the same time, I have not been uncritical; the knowledge and the research techniques that I describe are in a continual state of development. Even the general reader must appreciate the tentative nature of each link in the argument, and must make his own appraisals. Therefore much tabular and graphic material is reproduced, especially where critical differences exist among the leading scholars of the field.

The main line of population research for many years has been the development of satisfactory measurement procedures. Two fields have progressed: (1) data-collection procedures, and (2) statistical techniques for summarizing the data.

The success of this measurement phase now leads us into a new era of population research which seeks to comprehend the broader implications of population processes in social systems. On the one hand we would like to understand the influence of the social processes upon the population processes so as better to utilize our knowledge of social processes in predicting population processes. On the other, we wish to ascertain the impact of the population processes upon the social system—continuing the quest that Malthus stimulated.

In the new era of population research, social theory and mathematics are articulated with the existing population data and statistical procedures. On the side of social theory at least three disciplines are involved—economics, psychology, and sociology. On the side of mathematics at least three fields are encompassed—mathematical statistics, stochastic-process models, and design of computer systems.

This book is an introduction to the new era. The emphasis is placed upon articulation of population processes with sociological theory. But the treatment is everywhere constructed so as to be compatible with the contribution of the other five subject matters. Where compatibility is difficult to achieve care will be taken to clarify the issues at stake. Issues of substantive social theory are treated in the text, while mathematical issues are elaborated in the Appendix.

The book has two main parts. First, population processes are examined at the societal level, utilizing census and vital statistics data. Historical comparisons among Western nations are augmented by the recent non-Western data that permit cultural contrasts. By means of these data a critique of current generalizations is developed and an articulation with macro-level social theory can be stated.

In the second part of the book, data referring to the individual and the family as the social unit are used to augment the societal measures. Here the discussion is articulated with micro-level social theory. Fertility and migration are given an extended discussion. In order to demonstrate the compatibility of these two levels in the argument there is a theoretical chapter. The crucial theoretical development is not the statement of concepts but the demonstration that these concepts allow the various empirical generalizations to be stated compatibly and parsimoniously. Thus the main contribution of this book is the detailed study of empirical results with the aim of systematic theoretical interpretation.

It is hoped that this examination of relatively narrow aspects of social systems in depth will throw greater light on some of the broader aspects of social systems. There are, after all, very few characteristics of social systems sufficiently well measured to permit comparisons among nations and across historical time periods. Births, deaths, and migration are among the best measured of these characteristics.

CHAPTER 1

The Issues

ONE can gain insight into the present state of research and writing upon population problems through a historical review of its development. The classical issues were forcefully stated in the nineteenth century, especially in the controversy between the Malthusian and Marxist positions. These classical issues clearly arise out of a larger controversy over national social policy. Thus the classical issues are significant aspects of Enlightenment and post-Enlightenment intellectual history.

The nineteenth-century controversies have had lasting influence upon the policy contexts in which the population problem has emerged and upon the technical nature of population research. In the twentieth century the slowly accumulating bodies of data and of research techniques have led to a restatement of the technical nature of the problem—often summarized as the demographic transition.

Let us first find the roots of the nineteenth-century statement of the issues. Recall that the Enlightenment program for increasing human happiness rested upon the premises that (1) the method of science could discern the natural laws that governed the social system; (2) one could accordingly devise social reforms which would improve the system; and (3) a program of political reform could be instituted that would implement the scientifically derived social reforms.[1]

The position of Malthus is a contradiction of the second premise. The natural laws he propounded did not imply a program of meliorative social reform, but instead served to show that the goal of social reform could not be achieved. It follows in his position that all political action under the third premise is an exercise in futility. Thus Malthus turned the methods of the Enlightenment against the Enlightenment objectives.[2]

The position of Marx, in contrast, accepts the first and second premises of the Enlightenment but controverts the third. For Marx the program for reform cannot be achieved by tinkering with constitutions or even by political revolutions; the essential inadequacies of industrial society stem from the economic class relationships defined by the capitalist system, and it is these class relationships that must be changed before a program of social reform can be implemented.[3]

In order to see the implications of the controversy we must examine these arguments more closely. Malthus emphasizes the articulation of the social and biological factors in human social systems. On the one hand, a human society produces humans; on the other, the production of humans itself modifies the human society. For Malthus the production process has two components— births and deaths (migration is neglected as it can only be a short-run, local adjustment of the production process). Births and deaths are both biological processes that are influenced by social variables.

First consider births. To some extent controlled by customs of marriage and of sexual abstinence in all societies, births are nevertheless a consequence of "the passion between the sexes," a biological phenomenon that can be limited only to a small degree by custom. With calculations based upon human and animal populations Malthus shows that the influence of births alone upon the production system leads to a rapid rise in total population, a rise expressed by a geometric series.

Now consider deaths. Ultimately controlled by biological limits of aging, short of these limits they may be substantially affected by social variables through variations in the food supply, disease, and violence. The food supply provides an upper limit independent of the influence of the other two factors. The total food supply depends upon the biological characteristics of plants and animals as mediated by the agricultural resources of human society. It was Malthus' contention that the agricultural resources were essentially limited, thus preventing the plant and animal populations from attaining the geometric growth rates that would otherwise be implied by his argument for human growth. He considered the scarcity of arable land and the possible rate of improvement of yield from existing land due to technological change to be the two most important factors limiting the food supply. On the basis of calculations on the quantity and quality of land and on the likely technological improvement Malthus postulated an arithmetical increase in the food supply as an upper limit.

The joint implications of these two components are clear enough. If the death rate is governed only by aging and the food supply, then the geometric growth rates implied by births cannot be sustained. A geometric growth rate must be a short-run phenomenon to be subsequently compensated for by increasing death rates. Further, the mere shortage of food supply should lead to increases in deaths due to disease and violence long before actual starvation has achieved its full impact. These increases in deaths due to disease and violence would be accompanied by increases in the social ills that the reformers seek to eliminate.

Thus the joint implication of births and deaths is the cyclical recurrence of social ills. From the perspective of Malthus no social or political reform could remove the causes of these cyclically recurring social ills. The appearance of improvement would be a temporary illusion to be shattered by the reassertion of the limiting causes. These causes were rooted in biology and in the capacities of technology, neither of which were subject to political constraint.

In passing, one should note that Malthus' argument does not depend upon the existence of a single numerical expression that defines overpopulation in a human society —say a ratio of total population to total resources (either food supply or capital). He was able to reach his essential conclusions without entering into arid debates over the precise level of population density that the earth could sustain.

We should further note that political changes did occur in nineteenth-century Europe and that Malthus' gloomy prophecies were not upheld by the history of that era. Malthus survived as Scrooge in Dickens' *A Christmas Carol.*

Marx recognized the argument of Malthus (and of Darwin) as a serious alternative to his own and couched his remarks toward it in appropriate polemical invective. The appeal of the apparently inexorable biological laws in Malthus' system to those smitten by the achievements of natural science would obviously be great. Let us first indicate the points of disparity between Marx's own theories and those of Malthus.

Whereas Malthus relied upon biology to give his theoretical system an inflexible nature (reminding us of Freud), Marx relies upon technological change to give his theoretical system a dynamic character. For Marx the social laws were relative to each economic system, and each economic system was a consequence of its characteristic means of production, i.e., technology. Thus history is broken up into a sequence of relatively discrete stages, each one ushered in by innovations in technology. Within each such historical stage the essential social laws are to be discovered in the articulation between the class system and the economic system, the latter involving the production and distribution of commodities. According to Marx, the implications of the biological variables are relative to the particular historical stage. Thus the production and distribution of food is merely a special case of the production and distribution of commodities.

But now we see an essential difference in the approach of Marx. He was concerned with the *distribution* of commodities. The distribution of commodities is a result of the distribution of wealth. In turn the distribution of wealth is determined by the ownership of the means of production, and the ownership of the means of production defines the class system. The owners of the means of production control the political system and use it to their own ends. Marx sees these ends as the essential limits to production and the determinants of distribution, not the possibilities inherent in technological change. He regards the Malthusian argument on the influence of biological variables at the extreme (when all arable land is in use, for example) as remote from present reality, it is essentially an apology and an excuse for the immediate consequences of the class system.

Indeed, Marx argued that the appearance of a relative surplus population in industrial society served the class interests of the bourgeoisie and was aided and abetted by them. In order to drive down the price of labor (i.e., wages), an oversupply of labor must be created. This oversupply, the industrial reserve army, was fed by able-bodied males forced off the land by the capitalization of agriculture and its associated rapid technological change. These displaced peasants were augmented from several less stable sources of labor supply—women, children, the sick, and so on—each of them capable of entering the labor force for short periods of time sufficient to prevent the occurrence of a labor shortage that would force up the price of labor. (The influence of the division of labor and rising skill levels in allowing specific skills to come into short supply is insufficiently considered by Marx. I believe that the success of the craft unions is due to their recognition of these factors and their control of supply through apprenticeship.[4] However, "automation" might lead to a leveling of skill requirements during a period of adjustment of the education system, and leave a whole generation of adults facing the prospect of declining earnings).

If we take the prophecies of Marx literally, then he fared no better in history than Malthus. The test of prophecy would lead us to skip lightly over these two figures. But historical events in this century have revived the significance of their controversy; contemporary world history owes much of its cast to their analysis.

Toward the close of the nineteenth century, declining birth rates became increasingly evident in Western Europe, with the paradoxical result that the population-policy issue was the raising rather than the lowering of the number of births.[5] Political changes in Western Europe, such as the appearance of welfare legislation, had the effect of deflecting the revolutionary violence that Marx had envisioned.

Also toward the end of the nineteenth century the results of improved data collection were first felt in population analysis. Three independent sources of techniques were involved. The censuses, established for purposes of allocating taxes and votes, provided time series of population trends within several nations, notably Britain and Sweden. Public health research into the causes and controls of mortality led to the establishment of vital-statistics record systems that provided further estimates of trends. The needs of life insurance companies to estimate present and future mortality rates led to the development of a life table as a statistical summary of the mortality experience of a total population and as a tool for estimating trends in mortality. By the 1930's a new profession had emerged as the conjunction of these three techniques—demography.

During the twentieth century two major historical occurrences changed the nature of population problems. The Communist revolutions enshrined Marx as a social prophet and endowed his polemical critique of Malthus with dogmatic status, thus reviving ideological controversies that had long been dormant. At the same time, the political and economic influence of Western Europe brought about vast changes in the rest of the world, in particular a rapid drop in death rates, little change in birth rates, and a dramatic increase in total population. These events revived the Malthusian prophecies and analysis in full force.

Western demographers strove to summarize the available information on world population trends in a scheme called the Demographic Transition. Several versions of this scheme have been proposed from the 1920's through the 1950's. Considering birth rates and death rates alone (the approach of Malthus), three stages of historical experience are described. In Stage I the birth rates and death rates are high, perhaps canceling out the effects of each other in a cyclical pattern of growth and decline of total population, and sensitive to some degree to changes in technology as postulated by Malthus. In Stage II the death rates fall dramatically, yet the birth rates are relatively unchanged—and a Malthusian nightmare of population growth ensues. In Stage III the birth rates begin a dramatic decline, resulting in a population growth that is slowly increasing or declining—and the Malthusian dilemma is resolved.[6] [Figure 1-1]

The implications of the demographic transition are brought out more clearly if we describe the changes in the technological and economic order which accompany these modifications in birth and death rates. We would like to see how such changes affect the Malthusian concern for food production and the concern of Marx for distribution of wealth. More significant, however, are changes in scientific innovation, technological diffusion, industrial organization, bureaucratic management, and in the occupational structure, for these are the more

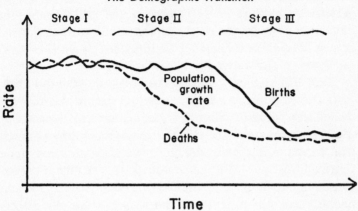

Figure 1-1

The Demographic Transition

basic changes that influenced the system of production and consumption in the West.

The timing of the technological developments in the West in the nineteenth century is quite curious. There was indeed a period of rural exodus, with Ireland serving as the most remarkable example even though unaffected by modern agricultural technology. But, after some delay, there arose such a great demand for labor in the developing industrial centers that ultimately it could not be met even by the rural surplus within the industrializing country. Labor moved great distances across national boundaries to fill this demand, from Europe to America and from Eastern Europe to Western Europe. From the point of view of the rapidly industrializing nation there was a relative underpopulation which was further accentuated by the fall in births. Evidently even Marx underestimated the scope and rapidity of technological change in Western society.

In order to comprehend the vast transformations that have taken place in the West and have been exported in various guises to the non-Western world, we need a more comprehensive theory of social change than either Malthus or Marx can provide. To simply seek a synthesis of these two positions would still be insufficient.

Our only source of appropriate social theory lies in the works of Max Weber.[7] Here we find an effort to elucidate the causes behind the great transformation of society in the West as contrasted with the relative absence of such transformations even in the highly developed civilizations centered outside the Western world. Weber analyzed the conditions leading to the breakdown of traditional society in the West. His analysis of the non-Western world was aimed at finding the conditions that inhibited the initial breakdown of traditional society in these countries. For our purposes we shall have to extend Weber's theory to take account of the conditions under which a non-Western country will accept the new technological and social forms from the West. The breakdown of traditional society in the non-Western world is in part a response to a diffusion process from the West and need not replicate in detail the breakdown that occurred in the West.

Weber augments the analysis of previous theorists by placing science and technology within a broader social context. In particular he identifies two constraints upon these sources of social change: First, a set of values and attitudes associated with traditional society which are antithetical to science—not merely opposed to science but indeed incompatible with science; and second, a set of managerial practices, a characteristic commitment to efficiency in the organization of work that Weber terms bureaucracy, within which the full scope and capacity of technological change is realized. Within modern bureaucracy a set of values and attitudes appropriate to science and technology emerge.

From this perspective we must attempt two tasks. First we must relate the breakdown of traditional society in the West to the course of the demographic transition in the West. Second we must relate the transformation of traditional society in the non-Western world to the demographic transition in the non-West.

To carry these tasks out we must first note that changes in mortality and fertility, in the West and in the non-West, are the result of the adoption of technological changes. In the next chapter we shall argue this point in detail. For the present we must view social systems from the perspective of their permeability to technological change, and the selectivity of their permeability to different aspects of technology. Herein lies the difference between the rate of effective adoption of mortality reducing technology and fertility reducing technology in the non-Western or "underdeveloped" nations.

In considering any particular technological innovation we must raise the classical questions of means and ends. We ask, What values or purposes do the people seek through adoption of technology? Mere availability of technology is an insufficient explanation for its use.

If we consider mortality alone then the relevant values in the West are those that emphasize preserving the lives of individuals. In a general way the cultural tradition of Christianity has given more significance to the individual than have the traditions of many other religious systems. However, the otherworldly emphasis of Christianity might be construed as an indifference to the preservation or extension of life—a fatalistic view. The Renaissance concept of the individual is more concerned with the present and with biological reality, perhaps setting a stage, in a general way, for the subsequent adoption of health programs.

Even given a rationale for the support of individual health, there is the question of the cultural basis for the public-health programs that extended the benefits of medical knowledge to the general public. One is inclined to believe that the powerful were interested in the health of the general public only to the extent that their own skins were involved. Thus one is not surprised to find great emphasis upon the control of contagious and infectious diseases. However, the extension of some other aspects of medical technology would seem to stem from the values of the medical professionals themselves.

The diffusion of health improvements to the non-Western world raises not only the issues above but also the question of the political relations between the West and non-West, namely colonialism. If outside political control is sufficiently strong, then certain kinds of technology can be introduced into a colony even though it is substantially at variance with the colony's indigenous culture.

With fertility the problem is much more complex. The relevant values are much more fugitive in their expression, save for the explicit positions taken by organized religion in recent time. Even here, however, one must qualify the discussion of values in terms of the particular technological means of achieving fertility control. Indeed, the diffusion of birth control clearly differs according to the specific technological means involved.

The technological means can be discussed in three groups.[8] First are certain means available widely before the advent of the industrial revolution, including abstention, *coitus interruptus*, and various physical and chemical efforts to either intrude directly upon sexual intercourse or to induce abortion. There is sufficient evidence for the existence and use of these methods but it is extremely difficult to ascertain the extent of the use, the effectiveness of the use, the differential use within a society, and the time trend in fertility as a result of increasing use or increasing effectiveness. In the matter of sterilization and abortion we can estimate use and effectiveness in some societies, but lacking any clear-cut alternative for the other methods we tend to assume that the influence on time trend of fertility is negligible.

Second are the means or devices that became widely available in Western Europe during the nineteenth century, especially condoms and jellies. Such devices are apparently responsible for the dramatic drop in fertility that occurred. Their availability at low cost is a by-product of the general process of industrialization in Western Europe. These means have two special characteristics which influence their effectiveness. Their successful use requires (1) some degree of collaboration and mutual agreement on the part of the husband and wife —a two-person decision process being necessary; and (2) constant, consistent, regular behavior patterns that imply not only a high motivation for success on the part of the users but also a highly compulsive self-control almost tantamount to a special personality syndrome.[9] Evidence for the existence and diffusion of these methods can be obtained from a variety of kinds of data. In the second and succeeding chapters we shall enter into a technical discussion of methods for estimating the effects of the diffusion process upon the time trends in fertility.

In the third category are means or devices newly developed or currently under development, especially the various oral contraceptives and the intrauterine devices. These means are designed to require less motivation and less compulsive regularity in their use while maintaining high levels of effectiveness; they might require less collaboration and also less mutual agreement between husband and wife, but this is a moot point. The effect of these techniques upon the future time trend can be estimated in part by the development of appropriate computer models.

The relevant religious and cultural values either oppose specific techniques of birth control or oppose low fertility itself. However, the religious and cultural values also contribute to the formation of personalities that are appropriate for the effective use of the means. It is this aspect of the value problem which was the focus of attention of Max Weber in his studies of the disintegration of traditional society in the West. Weber was not concerned directly with birth control but with the development of compulsive personality traits associated with an extreme commitment to efficiency and "rationality."

Let us have a brief stocktaking. We have reviewed the three major classical arguments in population—Malthus, Marx, and the Demographic Transition. We have noted shortcomings in these arguments as explanations of trends in the birth and death rates of various countries. Two supplementary arguments have been put forward to overcome the shortcomings of the classical arguments, namely the transition from traditional to modern society as described by Max Weber, and the diffusion of technology.

In the remainder of this book we shall develop a demographic theory that includes the arguments discussed above. This theory can be expressed in mathematical form and can be tested. The appropriate computer models are being developed in my current research. Throughout the book the theory will be developed as part of a close scrutiny of the results of previous empirical research.

A full-fledged mathematical discussion is beyond the scope of this book. Matrix algebra and stochastic process theory are needed to state these issues explicitly. A review of technical issues is given in the Appendix. Nevertheless, we must clearly state the substantive issues that determine the mathematical form of the theory. Thus we shall now introduce in the text a series of issues with which we shall grapple throughout the remainder of the book. These issues are of two types: (1) the kinds of variables that should enter into the theory, and (2) the kinds of *relationships* among the variables that should be expressed by the theory.

First let us consider a simple Malthusian accounting equation. We regard the change in total population of an area during an interval of time to be equal to the number of births minus the number of deaths during that interval of time. If the change in total population is C, and if the time interval is bounded by two successive points in time t_1 and t_2, with the number of births and deaths represented by B and D respectively, then we may write

$$C = B - D \qquad \text{(in the interval } t_2 - t_1)$$

From a Malthusian perspective, however, this accounting equation would be more illuminating if it took into account the age and sex composition of the population. To do this let us measure time intervals in years. Then we can see that the age at last birthday will be zero for all the births occurring in a single year and that the age at last birthday will exceed zero if the person was born in a previous year and has not died. To get into the age-zero category one must be born, and to get into the successive age categories one must survive. Thus the accounting equation need specify only a single annual number of births, but must specify the annual number of deaths by age at last birthday in order to measure the age composition.

To measure the sex composition as well, two numbers of births and two numbers of deaths must be specified for each age. In this form the accounting equation is best represented by a table (matrix) in which two separate columns represent the two sexes and successive rows represent the ages from zero to some terminal age, say ninety-nine. For any single year we now have two hundred accounting equations, one for each category of age and sex. The symbol C is used to indicate the age and sex category to which it refers; if it refers to age zero then $C = B$, but if it refers to any other age, then $C = -D$.

This accounting equation becomes more interesting if we utilize it to keep track of the age and sex composition of a population over a number of successive years. It then becomes apparent that the number of persons of a given age, say age x, depends upon the number of persons who were initially born x years ago and on the survivors in each subsequent year up until their present age. We are keeping track of the occurrence of two events and of a distribution of persons subject to these events. It is clear that the occurrence of the events (birth and death) depends to some degree upon the characteristics of the distribution of persons. But the distribution itself is the joint result of the occurrence of the events. We shall seek to clarify the relation between events and distribution by asking a new question.

How can we use the accounting equation for predicting population trends? We would have to reinterpret the accounting equation. A standard procedure is to obtain the numbers of births and deaths on the right of the accounting equation from other equations. The other equations contain two kinds of quantities: (1) probabilities of birth and of death, respectively, and (2) a population of persons who are subject to these probabilities, often called a "population at risk" by demographers (in stochastic processes a distribution vector). Thus the number of births in the first accounting equation equals the product of the probability of the births per person times the total population; the number of deaths becomes the product of the probability of deaths per person times the total population. In the interval $t_2 - t_1$,

$$B = \text{Probability (births)} \times \text{total population}$$
$$D = \text{Probability (deaths)} \times \text{total population}$$

One advantage of these new probabilistic equations is that we may now make separate assumptions as to the future state of the probability and of the population. The second quantity, the future population, is now very neatly handled. Suppose our prediction of the population trends begins at a time period for which we have actual empirical data. Call this time period the present. Now if the prediction begins at the present and runs into the future we may choose to enter the present population into our equation for our first computation. If we select birth and death probabilities that apply for the next time unit, say next year, then our equations will produce an estimated total population at the end of that year, for we merely add C to the present population (taking account of the sign of C). Proceeding year by year, our equations themselves will produce new total populations and we have only to supply new probabilities. In this way we represent the dependence of the total population upon two parameters—the probabilities of birth and of death respectively.

But the relationship between these two parameters is not so clear. As it stands, we have assumed that the events of birth and death are mutually exclusive in a given year (thus omitting infant mortality) and that the probability of death is independent of age (and therefore independent of year of birth). The latter difficulty can be removed if we introduce an age variable into the definition of the distribution of the population.

Let us give a probabilistic interpretation to the whole set of two hundred equations which take account of the distribution of the population by age and sex. The two parameters are now conditional probabilities, their numerical values differing according to the age and sex categories so that there are, in principle, two hundred birth probabilities and two hundred death probabilities. (In practice most of the birth probabilities are defined as zero, all except those for women in the age range in which reproduction is physiologically possible.)

We now have two parameters conditional upon two variables. As before, we can see that the distribution of the total population described by age and sex depends upon the probabilities of birth and of death. The distribution next year is obtained as a consequence of the probabilities for this year, but the distribution next year also depends upon this year's distribution, as these are the numbers that are multiplied by the probabilities. Since this year's distribution depends upon last year's probabilities, we see again that the distribution at any given time depends upon the previous history of probabilities for the population. Our probabilities are now dependent upon age and sex, the same variables that define the distribution. If we could specify the set of future probabilities, we could then calculate the implied future distribution of population.

Supplying the new probabilities is not so simple. We may continue to use the same probabilities in future years (assuming the probabilities are independent of time, or stationary). Otherwise we must specify equations with which we calculate the new probabilities. Introducing the age and sex variables into the definition of the distribution of the population has increased the number of equations, but it has also increased the merits of assuming that the probabilities do not change. We feel certain that the changing age and sex composition of the population would indeed yield changing numerical values of the probabilities of births or deaths over the undifferentiated total population, but the changing age and sex distribution should not influence the probabilities conditional upon age and sex.

Perhaps the future probabilities will depend upon additional variables. How shall we proceed to expand our equations? Here we clarify our substantive interpretation of these equations.

There are two different ways to interpret the probabilities of birth and of death in these equations. One is to regard these probabilities as averages that characterize the overall system under study. As these averages are independent of the total population, we multiply the averages times the total population in order to obtain the implied number of births and of deaths. This interpretation is called an aggregate or macro interpretation.

The other way to interpret the probabilities is at the micro level. The probabilities are associated with the individuals in the system. If the probabilities for each of the individuals are independent of the probabilities for all the other individuals then the probabilities for the total population are obtained by multiplying the individuals' probabilities. If the probabilities are not independent then we need to specify the form of the dependence. Either way, the micro approach commits us to specifying the individual probabilities; they have to be estimated or obtained from theoretical considerations.

Note however that the introduction of the age and sex variables into the problem differentiated the individuals in the population. By introducing further variables in the same way we would make our macro theory look more and more micro until it might seem useless to differentiate these two interpretations. The estimation of parameters would be much the same for both interpretations. However, if the parameters are related by equations that stem from theoretical considerations there might indeed be an important difference between the macro and micro perspectives.

The issues underlying the choice of micro or macro approach have bedeviled social science for more than a century. In this book we shall assert the need for a micro-level theory, a theory of the behavior of the individuals in the population, but we shall further argue that the behavior of the individuals is largely constrained by macro-level considerations. In Chapter 2 we shall review empirical research carried out from a macro perspective. But in Chapter 3 we shall discuss the micro perspective in greater detail, showing how it can be more effectively related to the macro perspective.

Now let us return to the problem of expanding the number of variables in our equations. There are two issues—how we do it, and when we should do it. Neither is easy to determine, but the second is more difficult than the first.

Let us indicate the general procedure for expanding, noting difficulties as we go. Note at the outset that there are considerable costs involved both in the increasing complexity of the equations and in the increasing difficulty of estimating the parameters.

Consider births. We can develop a list of possible variables to introduce (at our present understanding of the problem) by beginning with the occurrence of the event—a birth to a woman—and listing apparently pertinent characteristics of the event. Thus biological aspects of the female and of the male might appear first on our list, followed by psychological aspects of the female and of the male, and then by various social measures, including the present and previous experiences of the female and the male. The order in this list tells us nothing whatsoever about the significance or pertinence of the variables; it is just a convenient order for enumerating candidates for inclusion as variables. The actual list of variables enumerated will differ, depending upon who is doing it.

Now suppose we have such a hypothetical list and decide that one variable which has to be included is the area of residence of the mother. If we recognize three different areas then we have six hundred equations to contend with. For any given year we have to estimate the new parameters, the newly defined conditional probabilities. What, however, are we supposed to do with a woman who moves from one area to another? Is the parameter assigned to her the first area, the second area, a combination of the two areas, or a special parameter for "movers"? This problem can be most neatly resolved if we have a theory of the fertility behavior of women in which area is a variable, a theory that has been tested.

The difficulties brought in by the fact that people can change areas are typical when new social variables are included. Sex of individuals does not change, age of individuals changes in an orderly way, but the social variables admit of many possibilities of change that are as yet insufficiently well understood. In later chapters we shall review the present state of our knowledge.

A different problem emerges if the new social variable is measured over a different population from the one that is directly under study. For example, consider the possibility of migration into and out of the population whose future growth we are attempting to predict. We can consider the migration out as a characteristic of persons presently in our population, and therefore define migration probabilities that can be multiplied by a distribution of our population in order to predict future out migration. We can also specify the influence of the out migrants upon the probabilities of birth and death by adjusting our distribution appropriately (under the assumption that the out migration itself does not influence the probabilities of birth and death).

But when we consider migration into our population our previous methods break down. The distribution of potential inmovers has not yet been defined, and the probabilities of migration to our population have had little light shed upon them by the study of our own population. Further, the appropriate birth and death parameters for this in-migrant population are not known. Either we expand our scope to consider a larger system of populations or we must adopt some very messy procedures in order to take account of the influence of in-migration. In practical application today the degree of political control over international migration simplifies the statistical problems when the populations under study are nations. Regions within nations, however, are very difficult to treat as being free from in-migration.

We now note that the original accounting equations and the set of probabilistic equations should be enlarged to include migration as an event contributing directly to population size. Thus the change in population $C = B - D \pm M$. We shall not modify this accounting equation for the total population throughout the remainder of the book. But we will extend the detailed description of the distribution of the population and modify our probability equations accordingly. In extending the description of the distribution we will also find it necessary to define new probabilistic parameters to take account of the changing social characteristics of individuals—for example, social mobility.

The discussion above illustrates how one might expand the set of variables to be used in predicting future population. The question now at hand is, should we expand the set of variables?

In general one should never expand the set of variables unless explicit criteria can be introduced to show the insufficiency of the reduced set of variables. Of course, the direct procedure to demonstrate the insufficiency of a set of variables is to compare its performance with the performance of an expanded set of variables. But to compare the performance of the two sets of variables we need criteria.

There are several things to be said about these performance criteria. First of all, in our statement of the problem we are concerned that the equations predict total population growth. The introduction of age and sex variables is sufficiently justified by this criterion. However, if our purpose was the prediction of the age and sex distribution of the population we might reach different conclusions about the relative importance of variables. The comparison of methods cannot be made independently of the criteria—the criteria should define the numbers that are to be compared.

It is clear that the comparison of numbers from two sets of equations must be relative to certain empirical criteria as to the "goodness" of a prediction. These empirical criteria will be developed in part from past historical series of data and in part from the comparison of predictions year by year with new information. But the empirical evaluation is not independent of the purposes of the user of these equations. Even though an expanded set of variables would be "better" in some empirical sense we would still want to know, how much better? And is the improvement worth it?

There is a whole battery of classical statistical procedures for comparing the numerical values of the criteria between the two equations and with empirical data. In general these statistical techniques compare two characteristics of sets of numbers—the means and the variances. From this perspective one can compare the variances, say, associated with two sets of equations. One can determine the amount of additional variance "explained" by an additional variable. The additional variance can be compared with some measure of additional cost of including the variable in these equations.

It would be easy, however, to exaggerate the importance of the classical statistical tests as criteria. There are two main omissions from these procedures and only one real gain. The real gain is the elimination of redundancy in the set of equations. Frequently one variable serves to represent, or index, other variables sufficiently well for the purposes of prediction. If a variable has already gotten into our equations implicitly we may not wish to go to the trouble of making it explicit. Variables can enter implicitly either through the fact that the technique of measurement cannot separate out the effects of several variables clearly, or through the regularity of occurrence of the two variables together (the correlation) even though they are measured independently. Crudeness of measurement in part stems from deficiencies of measurement technique, but may also arise from the natural form in which the data is found or from an interaction between the measuring instrument and the data.

The omissions of the statistical methodology (when blindly used) are due first to the empirical aspects of the situation and second to the policy aspects. Both these aspects, however, derive in turn from what one might call the "dynamic" aspects of the problem.

On the empirical side one should never trust the apparent stability of relations among social variables. The ever-present influence of technological change is sufficient to warn us against such confidence. For a decade or more a simple set of equations may quite closely fit the data, yet changing social conditions may abruptly yield bad fits. Thus the "response" of the system of equations to social change must be a criterion, as well as the closeness of fit to a time series of data. A user may be able to tolerate some inaccuracy in fit if the equations correctly inform him of impending major change—serving a watchdog function and giving him useful predictions of the implications of this major change.

From this perspective one would want to include in one's equations variables that are sensitive to social change. Further, one should try to express relationships between the sensitive variables and the remaining variables that are appropriate to the possible kinds of social change. Discovering and expressing these relationships constitute the most critical task of social theory in our problem. The social changes themselves will be, for the most part, unanticipated in our equations. But we can seek to anticipate the effects of these changes.

There are two kinds of relations that one might use to take account of social change. First, some social changes may have the effect of modifying the distribution of population without modifying the probabilities in the equations. Thus the effect of wars upon births is largely to remove men from families, the same probabilities holding for those families that remain intact. Second, some social changes may directly alter the probabilities. These social changes are much more difficult to deal with.

From the policy perspective the anticipation of the effects of change is the primary purpose of the equations. The policy maker wants to know whether different policies might yield different results. To test different policies one must express the impact of various hypothetical kinds of social change in his equations.

Thus the policy maker is most concerned that impact of social change is adequately represented in the equations. To the extent that the user of classical statistics does not take account of social change he restricts the usefulness of his equations. Taking account of social change requires a knowledge of substantive theory and of its degree of confirmation. Further, this knowledge must be explicitly expressed in the system of equations, and must be taken into account in the comparison of two sets of equations.

With these strictures in hand we now turn to the task of testing additional variables for inclusion in our equations. In Chapter 2 we shall review the classic data summarized as aggregates by demographers. In this review we shall evaluate the classic theories in demography that we discussed in the beginning of this chapter. In particular we shall attempt to compare Western and non-Western historical experience.

In Chapter 3 we shall consider theoretical questions in more detail. In particular we will delve into the problem of the articulation between the macro and micro interpretations of our probabilistic equations. Thus we will be able to interpret psychological and social psychological data in our equations.

In subsequent chapters (4–6) we shall review data collected by psychological and social psychological techniques and test these data for inclusion in the equations.

NOTES

1. See Crane Brinton, *Ideas and Men* (Englewood Cliffs, N.J.: Prentice-Hall, 1963), Chap. 11.

2. Thomas Robert Malthus, *An Essay on Population* (2 vols.; London: Dent, 1960–61). There is a brief discussion of Malthusian theory in William Petersen, *Population* (New York: Macmillan, 1961), Chap. 17. For a brief history of population theory see Population Division, United Nations, *The Determinants and Consequences of Population Trends* (New York: United Nations, 1953), Chap. III, reprinted in Joseph J. Spengler and Otis Dudley Duncan (eds.), *Population Theory and Policy* (New York: Free Press, 1956), pp. 5–54.

3. See Ronald L. Meek (ed.), *Marx and Engels on Malthus* (London: Lawrence and Wishart, 1953).

4. See G. Renard and G. Weulersse, *Life and Work in Modern Europe* (New York: Knopf, 1926).

5. D. V. Glass, *Population Policies and Movements in Europe* (Oxford: Clarendon Press, 1940).

6. See Janet Abu-Lughod, "Urban-Rural Differences as a Function of the Demographic Transition: Egyptian Data and an Analytical Model," *American Journal of Sociology*, LXIX, No. 5 (March 1964), 476–80. There is a detailed discussion of the Demographic Transition on pp. 485–90. Also Donald Olen Cowgill, "The Theory of Population Growth Cycles," *American Journal of Sociology*, LV (September 1949), 163–70, reprinted in Spengler and Duncan, *op. cit.*, pp. 125–34.

7. Max Weber, *From Max Weber: Essays in Sociology*, trans. and ed. by H. H. Gerth and C. W. Mills (New York: Oxford U. P.,

1958); *The Protestant Ethic and the Spirit of Capitalism*, trans. by Talcott Parsons (New York: Scribner, 1958); *Wirtschaft und Gesellschaft* (Tübingen: Mohr, 1956). Weber's theories cannot be adequately understood from a reading of *The Protestant Ethic* alone. His ideas were further developed in a series of essays of which the most important were collected under the title *Wirtschaft und Gesellschaft*. The Gerth and Mills collection is a good translation of a limited selection of these writings.

    8. See Norman E. Himes, *Medical History of Contraception* (New York: Gamut Press, 1963).

    9. Gilbert Wheeler Beebe, *Contraception and Fertility in the Southern Appalachians* (Baltimore: Williams and Wilkins, 1942). In this book Beebe called attention to the significance of factors within the husband-wife relationship, especially communication, in the adoption and continued use of mechanical and chemical contraceptives.

CHAPTER 2

The Macro Data

IN this chapter we shall examine the historical pattern of birth and death rates in Western countries, and then examine these rates in the non-Western countries. For the West we have fairly good historical data for a century; the picture is reasonably clear; moreover, the corollary social processes are also reasonably well documented. For the non-Western case we have limited data, mostly recent. The problem of cultural variability —whether the plausible explanation of variation of these rates in the West has merit for non-Western countries —is not easily resolved. These birth and death rates change within the larger social context. We shall turn first to the diffusion of technological change in our interpretations of the data. But we shall also have to consider the impediments to the diffusion of technological change. These impediments stem in large part from the nature of traditional societies. Thus the Weberian problem of the breakup of traditional society will loom in the background of our analysis.

Let us review the standard interpretation of birth and death rates in the West, presenting summaries of the relevant evidence as we go. Mortality rates began to drop in the nineteenth century, accelerated their drop toward the end of the century, and then slowed their decline in the early twentieth century, apparently approaching an asymptote stemming from an upper limit on length of life.

The corollary social processes that have attracted attention are: (1) innovations in agricultural technology;

Figure 2–1

European Death Rates, 1800–1960

(Deaths per 1000 population per year)

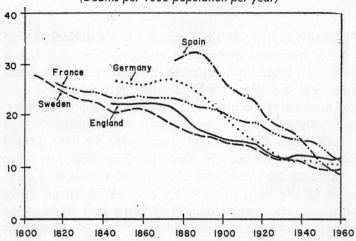

Sources: *Annuaire Statistique,* France, 1951; United Nations, *Demographic Yearbook,* 1963. Postwar rates for Germany are for the Federal Republic, excluding Berlin.

(2) innovations in public health and in medical technology—initially rather simple sanitation measures, subsequently the control of epidemics, recently the control of infectious diseases; (3) industrial advances making such products as cotton cloth widely available and therefore making possible changes of clothing; (4) relative international political stability, reducing deaths caused by military action and by the disturbance of economic and social processes. Reasons (1) and (2) made possible the rapid urbanization that took place; reason (3) is in part a by-product of urbanization, i.e., through the factory system.[1]

From a general perspective we note that the development of applied technology and of science play a major role in the mortality decline. Why did the benefits of these developments become widespread, diffusing throughout society (although somewhat unevenly)? In this instance the general values system, especially the religious system, placed great emphasis upon the preservation of life. The discontinuities in the diffusion of these benefits stem from differentials in occupational hazards and differentials in income; but the fact that epidemics affected all class levels doubtless encouraged the upper classes to support the early public health measures.

It is not easy to support these conjectures on the effects of general values and of class systems upon mortality. We shall return to this problem later in this chapter and again in Chapter 6.

The picture for fertility is somewhat more complex. Looking first at whole nations we see some evidence of moderate declines throughout the nineteenth century. There is, however, very clear evidence of a sharp decline in fertility during the period 1870–1900 that continues up through the 1930's. The sharp decline is most notice-

Figure 2–2
The Growth of Urban Populations, 1800–1960

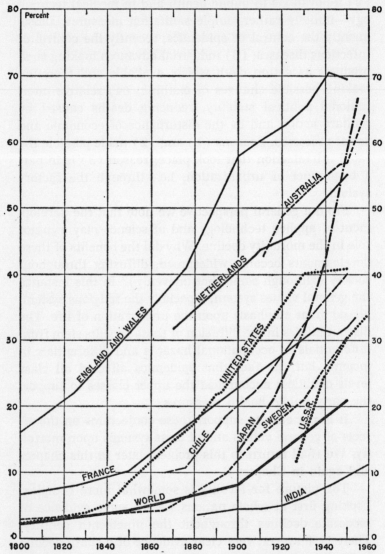

Source: Population Reference Bureau, *Population Bulletin*, XVI, No. 6 (September 1960) Fig. 1, p. 117. Data from United Nations, Bureau of Social Affairs, *Report on the World Social Situation* (New York, 1957), and other sources. Graph shows the per cent of total population living in localities of 20,000 or more. (The unit is 25 or more for the United States and Sweden.)

able in England, then appears in geographical neighbors (except Ireland).[2] The consensus of researchers is that a very slow trend toward the greater use and effectiveness of birth-control techniques was greatly accelerated by the activities of family-planning organizations, specifically as dramatized by the Bradlaugh-Besant trials in England in 1877.[3]

Figure 2–3

European Birth Rates, 1800–1960

(Births per 1000 population per year)

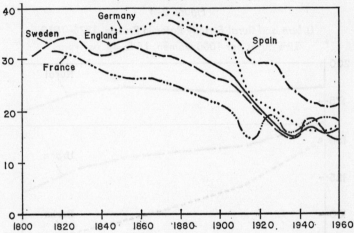

Sources: *Annuaire Statistique*, France, 1951; United Nations, *Demographic Yearbook*, 1963. Postwar rates for Germany are for the Federal Republic, excluding Berlin.

Further evidence for the diffusion interpretation is found by studying the differentials of fertility within the nations, especially the trends in these differentials. First let us examine the urban-rural differences. Urban rates, so far as we can see, dropped before rural rates; the lag in the decline of rural rates is often revealed in marked urban-rural differentials, but ultimately these differentials converge. This effect is brought out clearly in Prussian data from 1876 to 1910. A similar phenomenon is present in U.S. data, but we cannot document the initial declines of urban fertility rates. These data are consistent with a theory that the urban areas are centers of the diffusion process of adoption of birth-control techniques which proceeds with appropriate lags to the rural areas. Apparently this process has been going on a long time— certainly the difference between urban and rural birth rates at the beginning of this period suggests a substantial previous history for the process.[4]

Figure 2–4

Urban and Rural Fertility Rates in Prussia, 1876–1910
(Live births per 1000 women, 15 to 45, per year)

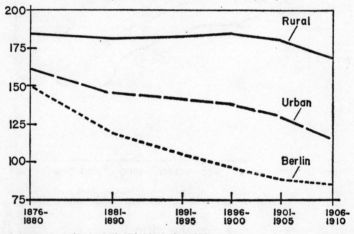

Source: *Preussischer Statistik*, Vol. 245, Berlin, 1914.

Fertility differentials by social class further illuminate the diffusion argument. Using occupation as our index we have a clear relationship with birth rates during the nineteenth century. The higher-status urban occupations have the smallest number of births, the lower-status rural occupations the largest number of births. The small-

Figure 2–5

Urban and Rural Fertility Rates in the United States, 1800–1950
(Number of children under 5 years old per 1000 white women
20 to 44 years old)

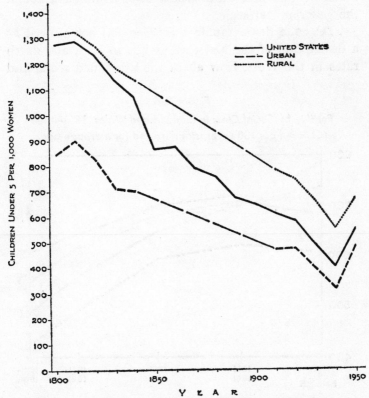

Source: Wilson H. Grabill, Clyde V. Kiser, Pascal Whelpton, *The Fertility of American Women* (New York: John Wiley and Sons, 1958), Figure 2, p. 18.

est number of births are found in the professional occupations, those with a high educational prerequisite.
This relationship, however, begins to change in the
twentieth century. The inverse relationship gradually
drops to zero and then becomes direct—the higher the

occupational status the higher the fertility. These data are consistent with the notion that the diffusion process originates with the urban professional classes and proceeds outward through the social scale as well as through the geographical scale.[5]

Thus the demographic transition has some merit as a description of the historical trends in birth and death rates in the West. How about the associated social and

Figure 2–6

Fertility by Social Class in England and Wales, 1851–1886
(Children per 100 wives, standardized for marriage age)

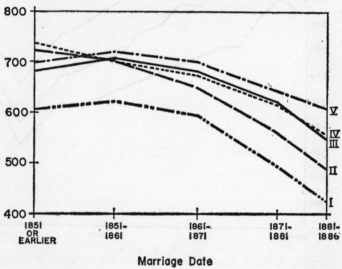

Marriage Date

Class I: Highly skilled and lucrative professional and business occupations—lawyers, capitalists, etc.
Class II: Less skilled and lucrative professional and business occupations—small shopkeepers, civil service type professionals, etc.
Class III: Manual laborers—Skilled.
Class IV: Manual laborers—Semiskilled
Class V: Manual laborers—Unskilled

Source: Adapted from John W. Innes, *Class Fertility Trends in England and Wales: 1876–1934* (Princeton, N.J.: Princeton University Press, 1938), Chart VI-B, p. 44.

Figure 2–7

Metropolitan London Area-Class Birth Rates, 1909–1934

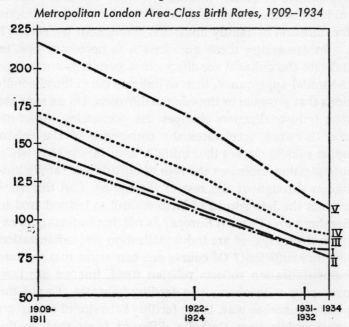

Source: Adapted from John W. Innes, *Class Fertility Trends in England and Wales: 1876–1934* (Princeton, N.J.: Princeton University Press, 1938), Chart XII, p. 100. Roman numerals on this graph refer to groupings of 39 London districts according to their relative socio-economic status.

economic processes in the West? Much attention has been given to urbanization and industrialization as correlated processes. From a diffusion point of view the former affects the geographical aspect directly through migration, while the latter affects the occupational structure through job mobility. However, the proponents of these two variables rarely indicate the theoretical relationships between either urbanization or industrialization and fertility. We shall consider the cultural content and processes.

The cultural content enters into the problem in two ways. First, what are the cultural conditions for the initial

appearance of family limitation among the urban upper
middle classes in a given society? What are the conditions
for diffusion of family limitation throughout the society?

In answering these questions it is necessary first to
indicate the cultural conditions that permit or encourage
the initial appearance, then to indicate the cultural conditions that promote or impede the diffusion. Let us suppose
that industrialization changes the occupation structure
and therefore accelerates the emergence of the urban
upper middle classes that initially limit family size, while
urbanization increases the rate of diffusion of family limitation throughout the rest of the nation. Can this view
explain the late spread of birth control to Ireland, and to
Southern and Eastern Europe? Is religion necessary to explain these lags, or are industrialization and urbanization
together sufficient? Of course one can argue that the late
industrialization reflects religion itself, but we are now
concerned with changes in fertility behavior. To put the
problem another way, is the fertility behavior of the urban
upper-middle-class Catholic different from that of the
urban upper-middle-class Protestant? American data suggest that the answer is yes,[6] but the number of generations of urban experience is much briefer for American
Catholics than for American Protestants, so that the
result is still not clear-cut. The fact that the Catholic
Church has an official position on family limitation is in
itself insufficient to demonstrate an effect of religion
upon fertility behavior.

The European birth rates after 1945 dramatically
underscore the insufficiency of all three variables to predict changes in fertility behavior. We can measure national fertility with the gross reproduction rate (and thus
remove the influence of age and sex). In 1960 the lowest

fertility in Europe was found in the following countries: Belgium, Sweden, Italy, Hungary, Rumania, Bulgaria, and Greece. The highest fertility was found in Ireland and Albania. The high countries are the most rural and the most orthodox (if we regard Communism as a religion). But the low countries include all levels of industrialization, urbanization, and religion. The explanation for the countries under Communist control is partly found in political and in doctrinal matters. With the waning of

Table 2-1 — Estimated gross reproduction rates for European countries, 1960*

Under 1.15	1.35–1.44
Belgium	Norway
Bulgaria	Poland
Greece	Scotland
Hungary	USSR
Italy	Yugoslavia
Luxembourg	
Rumania	**1.45–1.54**
Sweden	Netherlands
	Northern Ireland
1.15–1.24	Portugal
Czechoslovakia	
Denmark	**1.55–1.64**
East Germany	(None)
England and Wales	
Spain	**Over 1.65**
West Germany	Albania
	Ireland
1.25–1.34	
Austria	
Finland	
France	
Switzerland	

* Estimates, based on official and United Nations data, are from James W. Brackett and Earl E. Huyck, "The Objectives of Government Policies on Fertility Control in Eastern Europe," *Population Studies*, vol. XVI, no. 2 (November 1962), Figure 2.

Stalinism the orthodox Marxist opposition to Malthusian programs was sufficiently weakened that abortion clinics became legally sanctioned in all but Albania and East Germany. The national policies have varied within and among these countries between encouraging increased births and encouraging decreased births.[7] Nevertheless the births have dropped steadily from 1954 to 1960 implying a desire on the part of individuals to limit families —possibly stemming from a concern for the standard of living of self and of children. The explanation for low birth rates in Italy may be that the rapid industrialization and urbanization have offset the official religious views that discourage some techniques of birth control.

Other post-1945 data are not consistent with the simple interpretations of the influence of urbanization and industrialization. The so-called baby boom in the United States, Canada, and Holland was not anticipated by demographers. Efforts to comprehend this phenomenon have led demographers to place increasing stress upon social-psychological information. We shall review this recent research in Chapter 4.

The shortcomings of these macro-level explanations —industrialization, urbanization, and religion—may be partly offset by elaborating a micro-level explanation that takes the behavior of families into account. The most detailed and insightful discussion of the effects of the corollary social-psychological processes upon fertility declines is due to J. A. Banks.[8] He considers the factors surrounding the sharp decline in English birth rates initiated in the period 1870–1900. Since the decline first appears among the urban upper middle classes, especially the salaried professionals of London, Banks confines his attention to the social trends influencing these persons from 1840 to 1900. What economic and social influences upon these persons could lead to the desire to constrict fertility and to the acquisition of behavior patterns that in fact do constrict fertility? Banks constructs a theory of the planner's behavior that helps to explain the origin of the fertility decline in the West (also useful in our discussion of the baby boom).

Using historical documents for his empirical data, Banks develops the following argument. (1) In 1840 an upper-middle-class male could not marry until capable of supporting his wife properly according to his social station; husbands were much older than wives, and lengthy engagements were common. (2) From 1840 to the 1870's there was a long period of increasing prosperity—the number of jobs available in the upper-middle-class occupations increased and the financial returns from these jobs steadily increased. The result was a situation in which a son could, at marriage, attempt the same status-symbol display that his father was currently displaying; there was little or no temporary downward mobility as measured by size of home, neighborhood, number of servants, or style of carriage. (3) In the 1870's and 1880's the British economy leveled off; the upper middle classes did not suffer a loss of income but their subjectively estimated future income was no longer steadily rising and therefore could no longer support the same patterns of increasing status symbol display. (4) Faced with a need to rearrange their budgets, these people had a choice between maximizing the social-status display of their own selves or with maximizing the future status-symbol display of their children. Because these people could not transmit hereditary status to their children they transmitted occupational status by a definite cash investment in education; they opted in favor of maintaining the status of the children. (5) The cost of the child's education required that the number of children be restricted and that they be spaced. Such budgetary computations were undertaken by salaried parents. (6) The mechanism for restriction was made available by the contraceptive publicity following the Bradlaugh-Besant trials. (7) These people had the appropriate education, especially the women, to read and comprehend the family-planning literature.

The whole argument assumes that extremely calculating, rational decision making is indulged in by the urban upper middle class and that they are sufficiently compulsive in control of their own behavior that they can carry out the actions implied by their decisions, even to the extent of greatly modifying their sexual behavior. Banks supports this argument with his documentary data on budget construction. Further, we see that this is precisely the behavior pattern that Max Weber takes as the central syndrome in the development of modern capitalism. That the London salaried professionals would develop this syndrome seems likely from Weber's argument in *The Protestant Ethic and the Spirit of Capitalism*. The syndrome might initially appear in this group from religious sources, then diffuse throughout it.

Banks then argues that the pattern of family limitation diffuses through personal contacts and in response to prestige imitation motivation throughout society. This view is consistent with our earlier discussion of the correlation of fertility and social class. Note that the Banks argument can imply higher fertility for the upper classes in two ways: (1) Hereditary status of children is not so directly threatened by large numbers of children as is high occupational status; and (2) among planners the larger the income the larger the family if the desired standard of living for children is the same. Thus the hereditary upper classes and the wealthy upper classes can have relatively large families.

With the Banks argument we can attempt to interpret the influence of such variables as industrialization, urbanization, and religion through social psychological decision notions. In Chapter 3 we shall extend this type of theoretical argument and in Chapter 4 we shall introduce further evidence that is consistent with this view. Banks provides us with a theory of the behavior of family planners and with some clues as to the initial phases of the diffusion of family-planning behavior in the West. However, Banks provides few clues for the diffusion of planning practices in the non-Western world.

Now we wish to test our notions against non-Western data. Here we will find a far greater variety of social contexts within which the demographic changes might be introduced. Further, the patterns of more general social change are more varied in these cases. Therefore we shall turn aside from the strictly demographic aspects of social change and outline the more general theory of transition of a society from traditional social organization to rational-legal bureaucratic social organization that stems from the writing of Max Weber.

From the point of view of a Weberian theory of social change the drop in the birth rate is only one index of a very general social process. Indeed, the usual Weberian theory does not even deal with fertility or mortality. But it does consider the innovation and diffusion of technology in the context of the reorganization of the society and of the change in psychological characteristics of the society. The key reorganization of society is the emergence of rational bureaucratic forms of administration throughout the entire range of organized activities. Changes in law, religion, power relations, economic

structure, and education are all associated with the emergence of rational bureaucracy. The key change in psychological characteristics is the destruction of the traditional mode of orientation and its subsequent replacement
by a purposive-rational mode of orientation toward social
objects. Ordinarily the traditional mode of orientation is
broken up during widespread social disorganization, as a
substitute an outlook that we may call the short-run
hedonistic mode of orientation develops. The purposive-
rational mode of orientation emerges slowly and as a
result of special social conditions.

From this point of view we must differentiate two
kinds of "urbanization." The growth of urban population
due to the migration of surplus peasant populations is
quite a different social phenomenon from the growth of
urban population due to the demands of the industrial
labor market.

When we apply this type of analysis to the West we
must remember that it was the center of technological
and social innovation. For the non-Western countries we
must explain diffusion, but not innovation. Also we must
note that in the West a highly developed feudal system
was the social context for subsequent social change; the
social context varies for the non-Western nations.

Weber's own analysis was directed to the origins of
the purposive-rational mode of orientation and associated
bureaucratic forms rather than to the diffusion of these
phenomena. Consequently we will have to extend his
argument somewhat in order to use it in the present
discussion. In the origin problem Weber argues that the
emergence of novel psychological characteristics in the
West was a necessary precondition for the emergence of
bureaucracy and the specific form of capitalism in the
West. After the latter appeared, however, it was able to

spread itself, so the diffusion throughout the society or across generations did not wait upon prior psychological development; instead the new bureaucratic forms generated these psychological characteristics.

But can we expect the diffusion to jump boundaries that are both national and cultural if there is no subpopulation that can construct the first rational bureaucracy in the next nation? Some degree of receptivity to social change would seem to be a necessary prerequisite for diffusion.

The diffusion of new patterns of fertility control could result from the adoption of new practices by particular families, without any specific governmental or bureaucratic action, or could be directly stimulated by bureaucratic action. Or the diffusion could be hindered by bureaucratic action, or there could be several competing bureaucratic structures that stimulate and hinder the diffusion of birth control throughout the population. Thus we must take into account the mode of orientation of the individuals in the society as well as the bureaucratic structure and policy of the society. Further, the diffusion of fertility control might be part of the more general diffusion of Western technology, or it might be either selectively encouraged or discouraged.

The social issues in mortality reduction are far simpler than in fertility reduction. Thus we shall review mortality data first.

The causes of mortality reduction in non-Western countries are much the same as in the West. Basic public-health measures of sanitation and of epidemic control, especially in their effect upon infant mortality, have had the most significant effects. But the social context of mortality reduction in non-Western countries is quite different. The differences appear in the timing of the various modernizing social changes in the influences of the political system.

The differences in timing of social change result in part from the fact that the programs and technology that influence mortality reduction can be introduced into a society without modernizing it in any other way—indeed without the awareness of the general public. Thus there are no by-products from mortality reduction that enable the society to better cope with its other social problems, including those that stem from the mortality reduction itself. The psychology of the individuals in society may become less fatalistic in the long run, but there is no reason to expect it to become more like the psychology of the Western middle class as a result of mortality reduction alone. The comprehension of science and technology is not increased, nor is the growth of educational and research facilities. Industrialization is enhanced only to the extent that the reduction of adult illness (morbidity) yields a greater work capacity for a given size of industrial labor force—an exceedingly indirect effect.

The specific effects of the timing depend upon the political circumstances in which the public-health programs are introduced. In the administration of colonies the controlling Western nation often deliberately withheld industrialization, education, and other aspects of modernization yet introduced public-health programs—as, for example, in Indonesia.[9] In the case of the Communist leadership in Russia and in China,[10] programs of public health were introduced in the context of massive industrialization programs; neglect of agriculture and the use of starvation and murder to insure political control suggest that it was not an interest in persons as individuals but in persons as industrial laborers that motivated the public-health activities. Clearly such values differ markedly from those involved in Western mortality control. The non-Communist leaders in the non-Western countries found themselves in a great variety of situations, depending upon the previous experience of their countries—perhaps as colonies—and upon their programs of industrial development. Nevertheless, in all cases some degree of public-health activity has taken place, perhaps through the World Health Organization. These public-health activities were modeled on Western experience and had similar effects on mortality.

The shortage of good fertility data from the non-Western countries, plus the variation in characteristics of these areas, requires us to select a few nations and discuss each of them in some detail. The tables of birth rates for all such nations are not very useful. Three cases help us to interpret the recent declines of birth rates in traditional societies. These are India, Japan, and Puerto Rico. All three of these situations are covered in good monographs by demographers on the birth and death rates.[11] There are also numerous special surveys yielding information on the diffusion of technological knowledge and on social-psychological issues, as well as public programs intended to bring about change in the birth and death rates.

India, Japan, and Puerto Rico present contrasts in values, religious organization, and political systems. India has a heterogeneous religious composition but includes three large groups—Hindu, Buddhist, and Moslem. Japan has a relatively homogeneous religious composition, largely Buddhist in inspiration. Puerto Rico has a majority of Roman Catholics and a minority of Protestants. In all three cases the religious systems support "traditional" values.

But the nature of religious organization and its relation to the political system vary greatly. In India the heterogeneity of religion acts as a brake upon the political influence of the dominant religion, Hindu. It appears that the minority religions have developed more effective and more militant organization as a defensive posture than have the Hindus in their dominant position. Thus more effective political action may have its origin in the minority religions rather than in the majority religion. In contrast, the homogeneity of Japanese religion does not increase its political significance. In the Shintoist situation the religion was a prop for the feudal system symbolized in worship of the Emperor. Thus religion was not a source of power and influence independent of the political system; it was a completely subservient phenomenon. In Puerto Rico the dominant religion, Roman Catholicism, has been estranged from the political system; even though the bishops have been an independent source of influence, there have been marked limits on their ability to exercise influence when in direct conflict with the political leadership.

The political systems themselves are quite different in ways significant to our analysis. Japan has a highly centralized system, whereas India has a decentralized federal system. The relatively homogeneous cultural system of Japan tends to reinforce the centralized political system. Puerto Rico falls between the other two cases. In all three countries the "elites" are currently progressive in orientation. However, in Japan and Puerto Rico leadership comes largely from industrial and commercial figures, while in India a civil servant class performs similar functions.

In comparing the fertility experience of India, Japan, and Puerto Rico we might first consider a very simple explanation for the differences. Suppose we argue that

the initial reception of Western attitudes towards family
planning and the subsequent diffusion of these attitudes
are both simply the consequence of a general process of
Westernization of a country. Then we might expect that
India, Puerto Rico, and Japan would be the order of the
countries in terms of the degree to which they reflect
Western fertility patterns, since India has maintained
contact with England and France over three hundred
years, Puerto Rico maintained contact only with Spain,
a traditional society, until this century, and Japanese
contact began only a hundred years ago.

In fact, the degree of apparent Westernization of
fertility is exactly the opposite for these three countries.
Japan has moved rapidly into a Western pattern in recent
years, Puerto Rico has begun the shift to a Western

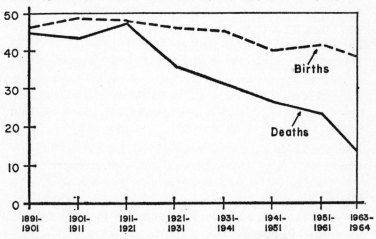

Figure 2–8

India: Birth and Death Rates, 1891–1964

(Average number of births and deaths per 1000 population per year)

Sources: S. Chandrasekhar, *Infant Mortality in India, 1901–1955* (London: Allen and
Unwin, 1959) Table 1, p. 56; United Nations, *Demographic Yearbook,* 1964.

Figure 2–9

Japan: Birth and Death Rates, 1901–1964

(Average number of births and deaths per 1000 population per year)

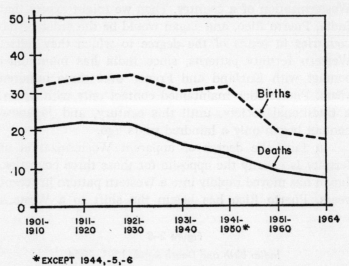

＊EXCEPT 1944,-5,-6

Sources: Japanese National Commission for Unesco, *Manual of Demographic Statistics in Japan;* United Nations, *Demographic Yearbook,* 1964.

pattern, and India has shown little indication of a Western pattern. So much for simple culture diffusion hypotheses.

The explanation for this paradoxical result lies primarily in the political variables, secondarily in economic variables. First let us note that the lowered fertility of Japan and Puerto Rico stems for the most part from the use of abortion and female sterilization rather than from the contraceptive methods used in the West. In both Puerto Rico and Japan the government has made these surgical methods possible, though in the face of religious opposition in Puerto Rico.

Religion has an independent influence only when

Figure 2–10

Puerto Rico: Birth and Death Rates, 1899–1964

(Average number of births and deaths per 1000 population per year)

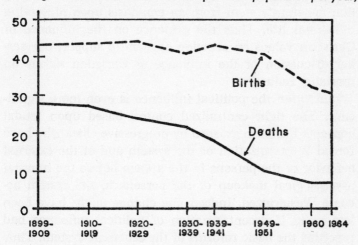

Sources: A. J. Jaffe, *People, Jobs and Economic Development* (New York: Free Press, 1959), Table 4.2, p. 56, Table 4.3, p. 61; United Nations, *Demographic Yearbook,* 1964.

(1) the objectives of the religious and political organizations run counter to each other, and (2) the religious organizations have an independent base of power. In Western Europe both conditions have often held, but this is an unusual state of affairs. Ordinarily the political organizations will defeat and control the religious organizations, making them subservient to political purposes. The most obvious case for conflict between religious and political organizations arises in the transition to industrial society. In this situation, religious organizations have become accustomed to propping up the feudal system and find themselves at variance with the programs and objectives of progressive political elites. However, there does seem to be a clear-cut difference between

Christian values in all societies and non-Christian values in the degree to which abortion is not accepted as a proper method of birth control. These objections to abortion apparently stem from an emphasis upon preserving individual life. Thus the evidence on the influence of Christian values on abortion appears to support our earlier discussion of the influence of Christian values on mortality reduction.

In Japan the political influence is even more significant. The tight centralized control based upon feudal concepts has been grasped by progressive elites who have forced Westernization of the system and of the external behavior of the persons in the system before the internal psychological makeup of the persons in the system became Westernized. Indeed, the change might have been less rapid if decentralization of political influence had preceded the basic reforms of the economic system. Thus we see the overriding significance of the political variables for the change of the total system.

Where the centralized political control is not as strong as in Japan the significance of the family decision units looms larger. This is especially true if traditional religion is losing its grip upon the people. Here again we must

Table 2-2 — Japan: Gross reproduction rates, prefectures by industrial type, 1925–1955*

Areas	1925	1930	1947	1950	1955
All Japan	2.6	2.4	2.2	1.8	1.2
Metropolitan	2.1	1.9	1.8	1.5	0.9
Other industrial	2.4	2.1	2.0	1.7	1.0
Intermediate	2.6	2.4	2.2	1.8	1.2
Agricultural	2.8	2.7	2.3	2.0	1.4
Hokkaido	3.1	2.9	2.4	2.3	1.4

* Irene B. Taeuber, *The Population of Japan* (Princeton, N. J.: Princeton U. P., 1958), p. 246.

differentiate the decision processes of the urban upper middle classes from the decision processes of the peasants. We must see where the pertinent decision processes in non-Western countries differ from those of the West. Then we can determine the different characteristics of the diffusion of family planning in non-Western countries.

Table 2-3 — Japan: The practice of contraception, 1950, 1952, and 1955‡

| | PER CENT REPORTING PRACTICE | | | INCREASE, 1950–55 | | | |
| | | | | Amount | | Per cent | |
Area	1950	1952	1955	1950– 1952	1952– 1955	1950– 1952	1952– 1955
				Present practice			
All Japan	19.5	26.3	33.6	6.8	7.3	34.9	27.8
Six cities	23.7	34.8	37.7	11.1	2.9	46.8	8.3
Other *shi**	23.6	31.1	34.0	7.5	2.9	31.8	9.3
Gun†	17.4	22.1	31.9	4.6	9.8	38.5	44.3
				Ever practiced			
All Japan	29.1	40.2	52.5	11.1	12.3	38.1	30.6
Six cities	35.7	52.0	56.6	16.3	4.6	45.7	8.8
Other *shi**	32.9	46.0	52.9	13.1	6.9	39.8	15.0
Gun†	26.6	34.6	50.8	8.0	16.2	30.1	46.8

* *Shi* are unincorporated municipalities, generally with populations greater than 30,000.

† *Gun* are districts that include all territory not *shi*.

‡ Irene B. Taeuber, *The Population of Japan* (Princeton, N. J.: Princeton U. P., 1958), p. 273.

The relation of urbanization and industrialization to fertility in non-Western nations has some similarities to those in the West, though subject to the political qualifications above. There is evidence that preindustrial cities have patterns of birth rates that are essentially similar to those in their rural hinterlands. This view has been most

Table 2-4 — Puerto Rico: Fertility differentials, 1955*

(Average number of children ever born alive, per woman)

Age	Total	0–4	5–9	10+	Urban Resi- dence	Rural Resi- dence	In Labor Force	Not in Labor Force
14 to 19 years	0.13	0.24	0.10	0.05	0.11	0.15	0.12	0.13
20 to 24 years	1.46	1.91	1.64	0.59	1.24	1.66	0.89	1.77
25 to 34 years	3.41	4.24	3.12	1.62	2.75	4.06	2.68	3.74
35 to 44 years	5.42	6.21	4.73	2.37	4.10	6.62	4.48	5.81
45 years and over	6.03	6.50	4.71	2.57	4.98	7.13	4.89	6.23

Column group "YEARS OF SCHOOL COMPLETED" spans Total, 0–4, 5–9, 10+.

* A. J. Jaffe, *People, Jobs and Economic Development* (New York: Free Press, 1959), Table 10.1, p. 179.

eloquently put by Abu-Lughod[12] with reference to Cairo, but it also seems sustained by much data from India. Driver[13] found no difference in births in central India by area of residence, while the Mysore study[14] found lowered birth rates in Bangalore City but uniform birth rates in the other towns and villages. Moreover, these studies and many others reveal that knowledge of birth control, while very thinly distributed, is nevertheless concentrated in the urban professional classes. Where differential births are initially revealed, they are best indexed by wife's education.[15] Thus "modernization" similar to that described by Banks for Victorian England seems to influence the lowering of fertility in non-Western countries, and seems to account for the relation to urbanization and industrialization.

Returning to the case of Japan, we see that the methods of birth control that reduced fertility have different decision implications from those used in the West. Let us note the special characteristics of abortion and female sterilization that differentiate them from Western methods of birth control and therefore make the theories of Banks less applicable to the problem of diffusion of fertility reduction to the non-Western countries. First, the female alone is required to act in order to prevent the birth by these methods, thus obviating the need to motivate or involve the husband in the decision. Second, the female does not have to understand any of the medical terminology involved; she has only to find her way to the relevant clinic. Third, the special motivations of mothers for limiting family size have overriding significance in the decision to use the clinic, motivations being at their peak for the mother with several previous chil-

Table 2-5 — Abortion in Japan, 1950–1954*

(The incidence of reported induced abortions, by age of women)

Age of women	1950	1951	1952ᵃ	1953	1954
			Abortions per 1,000 women		
All womenᵇ	23.1	29.6	36.3	47.7	49.8
15–19	4.0	4.7	3.8	3.9	3.7
20–24	28.3	37.5	33.3	42.6	43.4
25–29			57.2	76.9	80.7
30–34	39.4	49.7	65.9	88.0	92.1
35–39			59.2	76.7	81.3
40–44	20.3	14.5	32.5	41.4	42.2
45–49			4.2	5.7	5.7
			Abortions per 1,000 live births		
All women	209	299	398	572	646
15–19	302	441	432	525	571
20–24	144	212	254	351	381
25–29			278	399	445
30–34	279	391	443	663	773
35–39			765	1,172	1,437
40–44	592	879	1,411	2,259	2,826
45–49			3,149	4,877	5,984

ᵃ Percentage distribution for July-December applied to the total number reported for the year.

ᵇ All abortions related to numbers of women aged 15–49.

* Irene B. Taeuber, *The Population of Japan* (Princeton, N. J., Princeton U. P., 1958), Table 108, p. 277.

dren. Fourth, the diffusion of the relevant information need take place among women alone. Thus special attention must be placed on these channels of communication in order to bring about diffusion of these techniques of fertility reduction.

Male sterilization has been used in experimental programs in India. The vasectomy operation is ordinarily offered only to fathers with previous children. Enthusiasm for the vasectomy partly stems from the possibility of a subsequent operation that could restore reproduction. Consequently the fertility reduction implications of the vasectomy are unclear. However, there is some evidence that very small financial inducements are sufficient to attract males to the operation, suggesting that the level of male motivation for additional children is slight.[16]

Other techniques of birth control now coming into use require action by the female alone—the oral contraceptives and the intrauterine devices. These methods may meet less religious resistance than abortion and sterilization. From the point of view of population policy, however, the "female only" decision process has several liabilities. First, the fact that motivation for the female is greatest after several previous childbirths suggests that even extensive use of these methods could still imply substantial population increase. Second, the fact that detailed family-budget accounting is not associated with family planning suggests that spacing of children and other family activities will not be geared to social-mobility aspirations for the children. In other words, such methods may limit family size and thus alleviate population pressure on the total economy, but they might not destroy the forces against modernization within the household itself.

Clearly, family-size limitation and family planning are two separable processes. As we see above, family-size limitation can be brought about by the female or male alone, but family planning refers to the joint decision process of husband and wife in which certain family goals are determined and the necessary means to obtain these goals are selected. In those societies in which consensual families prevail (Jamaica)[17] or in which the stable monogamous unit is supported neither by custom nor by law, then family planning cannot take place. Family-size limitation by females is the only hope to slow population growth in this situation. The alternative of family-size limitation by males is extremely unlikely in the unstable family, for the footloose male will not feel the consequences of excess children personally and he is not likely to care about overall economic growth. The vasectomy may attract fathers, but why should it attract others?

Now let us consider a traditional society in which the stable monogamous family is supported by customs and laws. As a decision unit this family will have severe limitations. The extreme segregation of male and female roles has the effect of restricting the communication between husband and wife which is essential to joint decision making. The customs of the traditional village support a rigid division of labor and corollary partition of decision making among husband and wife, perhaps making for greater marital harmony by providing fewer opportunities for friction, but serving as a staunch barrier against social change. This situation is most clearly illuminated by the study of Hill, Stycos, and Back in Puerto Rico.[18] Family planning is better predicted by communication between husband and wife than by any other variable.

Now let us see how the diffusion processes depend upon these decision processes. There is substantial evidence that diffusion from a particular clinic or agency to the general population depends upon networks of interpersonal contacts. Mass media may also be involved, depending upon the political system and the literacy of the population. But there is every reason to believe that personal networks have the same importance here as they have in every other instance of adoption of technological innovation. In particular, the decisive contacts are the fairly close personal contacts.[19] Research by Keyfitz on the French Canadian family-size distributions supports this point of view.[20]

Within a city the personal contacts are in part segregated by social class, as we suggested in our earlier discussion of the Western countries. Within a village all persons may be connected by dense interpersonal networks. How are cities connected to cities, cities to villages, and villages to villages?

One answer is migration between these areas. But here we have a pronounced difference for men and women in traditional societies. Aside from the possibility of local markets connecting the villages, there is little chance for women to migrate from village to village. Thus female-oriented methods of birth control might not diffuse from a central village to surrounding villages; a clinic will have to be provided in each village and each clinic would start from scratch with its own clientele.

Use of birth control, however, might be diffused in part through the male migration patterns. In the U.S. knowledge of birth-control techniques is diffused among males in the armed services.

The scattered data that we have available on traditional society does not suggest a rapid diffusion of birth control in advance of a more general technological transformation of the society. From India, Egypt, and the differential fertility within Israel,[21] as well as Japan and Puerto Rico, we see evidence of this point. Yet the more general technology seems to index a disruption of the traditional social organization. This disruption might permit the diffusion of birth control, or it might not. Even if birth control is accepted we still have to know the extent and nature of the family-planning practices that guide its use.

In those instances where efforts have been made to diffuse birth-control practices throughout a traditional society prior to more general technological change, the results have been disappointing. The social and psychological impediments mentioned in the last few pages seem to exert a strong influence. The peasant village resists not only the technology but also the psychological transformations that would be appropriate to the use of the technology. Even when the technology is developed specifically to overcome psychological impediments, as with oral contraceptives and intrauterine devices, there remains the problem of motivation to achieve family-size goals. Lack of motivation may stem from a peasant's eye view of economic realities. Large families may not be a psychologically salient loss or inconvenience, and many sons may represent a gain.

If the theory of Banks predicts the emergence of small families in non-Western societies, then parents' social aspirations must be rising, especially aspirations for their children. These rising aspirations are a prerequisite for Western-style family planning. Furthermore, these aspirations must influence long-range budget-making behavior. Thus even with widespread use of better methods of birth control, four children may remain an ideal family size, implying substantial population growth.

Let us now review the demographic transition as a summary of historical trends in world birth and death rates. For the West the summary is quite useful. Many nations, despite a variety of fluctuations in birth and death rates, experienced substantial declines in both during the nineteenth and early twentieth centuries. These declines in rates first greatly accelerated population growth, then greatly decelerated population growth; the effect of the drop in death rates was strong at first, then the drop in birth rates came to predominate. This generalization best fitted those nations that were industrializing; public-health measures were followed by drug technology in reducing deaths, birth-control technology apparently spreading from urban professional classes reduced births. Minor exceptions include Ireland, where delayed marriage and celibacy reduced births long before industrialization, and France, where a long gradual decline in births was sustained in contrast to more precipitous drops elsewhere. By mid-twentieth century the least industrialized countries of Europe and of European emigrants were conforming to the earlier pattern. Once the major declines occurred, however, a new and more subtle relation between birth rates and social variables emerged; economic and political fluctuations appeared to have an impact on births, yet their influence was difficult to unravel in detail.

In non-Western nations the demographic transition has also been observed. The precise pattern of decline of rates, their initiation and the speed with which they proceed, is subject to great variation; political, cultural, and economic variables all influence these declines in complex ways. Nevertheless, accelerated population growth is widespread in these nations, and frequently threatens the entire basis for economic growth.

In summary, we wish to decide which social variables might be included in population-prediction equations. We can conclude that these variables must enable us to predict two social processes: (1) the diffusion of birth-control technology, and (2) the growth of the family-planning context within which birth control is used. We can borrow the experience of other types of technological change for (1), and we can extend the theory of planning behavior of Banks for (2). For both processes we can turn to the more general theories of Weber.

In Chapter 3 we shall discuss how to incorporate these variables in a formal theory, and shall provisionally state such a theory. Then in Chapter 4 we shall examine this theory in the light of more detailed evidence, especially social psychological data.

NOTES

1. Warren S. Thompson, *Population Problems*, 4th ed. (New York: McGraw-Hill, 1953), Chap. 5.

2. See John Anthony O'Brien, *The Vanishing Irish* (New York: McGraw-Hill, 1953).

3. See J. A. Banks, *Prosperity and Parenthood* (London: Routledge, 1954).

4. See, for example, Joseph J. Spengler, *France Faces Depopulation* (Durham, N.C.: Duke U. P., 1938), pp. 82–8, 101; Wilson H. Grabill, Clyde V. Kiser, and Pascal K. Whelpton, *The Fertility of American Women* (New York: Wiley, 1958), pp. 16–19.

5. D. V. Glass and E. Grebenik, *The Trend and Pattern of Fertility in Great Britain* (London: H. M. Stationery Office, 1954); Grabill, Kiser, and Whelpton, *op. cit.*, Chap. 5; John W. Innes, *Class Fertility Trends in England and Wales 1876–1934* (Princeton, N.J.: Princeton U. P., 1938); Spengler, *op. cit.*, pp. 86–100, 102.

6. See Ronald Freedman, David Goldberg, and Doris Slesinger, "Current Fertility Expectations of Married Couples in the United States," *Population Index*, XXIX, No. 4 (October 1963), 366–91;

Charles F. Westoff, Robert G. Potter, and Philip C. Sagi, "Some Selected Findings of the Princeton Fertility Study: 1963," *Demography*, I, No. 1 (1964), 130–5; "College Study Reports," *Population Bulletin*, XI, No. 4 (June 1955), XII, No. 6 (October 1956).

7. James W. Brackett and Earl E. Huyck, "The Objectives of Government Policies on Fertility Control in Eastern Europe," *Population Studies*, XVI, No. 2 (November 1962), 134–46.

8. Banks, *op. cit.*

9. Justus M. van der Kroef, "Population Pressure and Economic Development in Indonesia," *American Journal of Economics and Sociology*, XII (July 1953), 355–71; reprinted in Spengler and Otis Duncan (eds.), *Demographic Analysis* (New York: Free Press, 1956).

10. William Petersen, *Population* (New York: Macmillan, 1961), Chap. 15; H. Yuan Tien, "Birth Control in Mainland China: Ideology and Politics," *Milbank Memorial Fund Quarterly*, XLI, No. 3 (July 1963), 269–90.

11. Kingsley Davis, *The Population of India and Pakistan* (Princeton, N.J.: Princeton U. P., 1951); A. J. Jaffe, *People, Jobs and Economic Development* [Puerto Rico] (New York: Free Press, 1959); Irene B. Taeuber, *The Population of Japan* (Princeton, N.J.: Princeton U. P., 1958).

12. Janet Abu-Lughod, "Urban-Rural Differences as a Function of the Demographic Transition: Egyptian Data and an Analytic Model," *American Journal of Sociology*, LXIX, No. 5 (March 1964), 476–90.

13. Edwin C. Driver, *Differential Fertility in Central India* (Princeton, N.J.: Princeton U. P., 1963).

14. United Nations, *The Mysore Population Study* (New York: The United Nations, 1962), p. 84.

15. See Chapter 4.

16. See R. A. Gopalasami, "Family Planning: Outlook for Government Action in India," in Clyde V. Kiser, *Research in Family Planning* (Princeton, N.J.: Princeton U. P., 1962).

17. J. Mayone Stycos and Kurt W. Back, *The Survey Under Unusual Conditions: The Jamaica Human Fertility Investigation* (Ithaca, N.Y.: Society for Applied Anthropology, 1959), Monograph 1.

18. Reuben Hill, J. Mayone Stycos, and Kurt Back, *The Family and Population Control* (Chapel Hill, N.C.: U. of North Carolina Press, 1959).

19. Bernard Berelson, "On Family Planning Communication," *Demography*, I, No. 1 (1964), 94–105; Donald J. Bogue, "The Demographic Breakthrough: From Projection to Control," *Popu-*

lation Index, XXX, No. 4 (October 1964), 449–54; Ronald Freedman, "The Transition from High Fertility to Low Fertility: Challenge to Demographers," *Population Index,* XXXI, No. 4 (October 1965), 417–29.

20. Nathan Keyfitz, "A Factorial Arrangement of Comparisons of Family Size," *American Journal of Sociology,* LVIII (March 1953), 470–9, reprinted in P. K. Hatt and A. J. Reiss, Jr. (eds.), *Cities and Society* (New York: Free Press, 1957).

21. Lois K. Cohen, *Decision Theory and Fertility as Applied to the Jewish Inhabitants of Palestine and Israel,* M.S. thesis, Purdue University, August 1961.

CHAPTER 3

Theoretical Development

WE argued in Chapter 2 that the demographic transition was a consequence of technological diffusion throughout society. Thus changes in mortality and fertility were viewed as aspects of the broad social changes resulting from rapid technological changes in the West. The diffusion interpretation was augmented along two theoretical lines. The theory of J. A. Banks was used to explain the social correlates of the initial diffusion of effective birth-control methods in the West. The view of modernization held by Max Weber was used to interpret technological diffusion in Western and in non-Western countries.

The discussion has served mainly to introduce plausible explanations for some historical demographic changes.

Can these explanations be made more systematic and rigorous? The present chapter will be devoted to this task.

We shall develop a way of stating the appropriate theories. The following three chapters will be devoted to a more detailed review of empirical research on fertility, migration, and mortality respectively in the light of this theoretical perspective. In this chapter we shall extend our discussion of micro and macro theoretical perspectives that began in Chapter 1. We shall specify the psychological content of the theory as well as the social constraints upon individual behavior.

Before stating such a theory we should indicate the purposes it should serve. These purposes will provide us with criteria against which to evaluate the theory that follows.

First of all we have the classic purposes of any theory —parsimonious statement, deductive character, and testability. Further, we wish to make predictions—statements about the occurrence of events in time. In our particular case we select certain events to be viewed as outcomes of social systems—births, deaths, and migration. We shall describe the social system in a way that will be most helpful in predicting the particular outcome under study. Thus our description of the social system may be different for different outcomes. No matter which outcome is under study, however, there will be similarities in the procedure for theory construction and similar problems that must be solved.

Our prediction of outcomes must be sensitive to major social changes. We want a theory that will guide us in predicting outcomes from the social system when the social system itself is undergoing change. Short-run prediction assuming the absence of change is not sufficient for our purposes. Therefore crucial tests of our theory will come from those historical situations in which vast social transformations have taken place or are taking place.

All three of the outcomes considered in this book are events measured as characteristics of individuals. Thus our theory must specify the relevant individuals. But our attention is focused on the aggregate outcomes, total births, total deaths, and total moves in a time interval. We introduce individual characteristics in order to improve predictions for aggregates of persons. However, we cannot include individual characteristics *ad infinitum*; there must be explicit empirical justification for complicating the theory.

It is possible to include individual characteristics without making explicit reference to social theories of individual behavior. The population can be endlessly cross-classified, as stated in Chapter 1. But this procedure does not ordinarily supply us with a theory that can predict the effects of change. Rather it provides us with certain regularities that are assumed not to change. These regularities are expressed as probabilities. In studies of mortality we see such methods in common use, but we also note that they omit such matters as the diffusion of new medical technology (save for fairly crude estimates) and the objectives of the political leadership of a country. The assumption of fixed probabilities may not suffice to account for social change.

When dealing with both fertility and migration we seek to evaluate change as a factor in social theories of individual behavior. For fertility we want to predict to whom the new technology diffuses in a population and then to predict the behavior of those who use the new technology. The probabilities associated with the users of the new technology bear little relation to the previous probabilities for nonusers. The evidence from Chapter 2 does not sustain the view that births can be predicted from the same variables after the demographic transition as before.

We wish to use psychology to obtain specific ways of relating individual characteristics to our outcomes. In our efforts to anticipate the effects of change we can use psychological theory and data obtained by psychological measurements.

We can use psychological theory in two ways even in the absence of psychological measurements. First, we can argue that certain variables, such as occupation, are strongly correlated with the relevant psychological variables, and that they can therefore stand in our equations as indices or surrogates for the psychological variables. Such indexing variables would have to be well measured in the society, as in a census, if they are to help. Second, we can argue that the form of our equations is in part dictated by psychological theory—the relations among the parameters themselves. This latter approach has been characteristic of classical economics. Given the maximization of utility as a psychological theory, a variety of aggregate conclusions have been deduced.

We employ such psychological theories in order to represent the "subjective" aspect of an individual's behavior; we view his behavior as conditional upon his own experiences, motives, and perceptions rather than on ours. We may introduce such variables as occupation on the grounds that the special biases in experience and perception of the individuals we wish to represent in our equations are correlated with occupation. When we propose a particular form of the prediction equations we can argue that the "subjective" aspect of behavior is appropriately expressed; thus we may represent a particular theory of individual learning in our equations.

The subjective aspect of individual behavior is often viewed in part as the outcome of a long history of stimuli experienced by an individual. Of these stimuli, those that result from contacts with other individuals are often viewed as very significant; in particular, the communication among individuals is given great weight. Such social communication can be, to a degree, indexed by social variables.

When we use psychological measurements it is ordinarily to obtain more accurate estimates of the "subjective" situation than is possible with the social correlates. Of course, one can evaluate the merits of using social correlates as indices for psychological variables by carrying out the measurement. However, care must be taken to assure that such correlations are not simply temporary phenomena. Psychological measurements may also help to clarify the processes by which subjective phenomena are created—in particular the social learning processes. In the long run this second aspect is more important, for we are far better off if we can predict future attitude formation than if we know only today's attitude.

The problems of measurement of psychological variables in large social systems are so great that the use of other variables as indices is often preferred even though the psychological variables are explicit in the theory. The costs of measurement of psychological variables are ordinarily prohibitive. Moreover, the error associated with the measurement is likely to be large and difficult to estimate. Thus we may prefer to use psychological variables either for deduction, as in the classic utility theory of economics, or for interpretation of the explanatory power of better measured variables (the indexing variables).

The additional explanatory power of psychological variables after social variables have been introduced into the analysis is often slight (as we shall see in Chapter 4). This situation may result from the high correlation of the two kinds of variables, or from the inherent liabilities in a strictly psychological explanation of certain kinds of behavior.

Let us amplify the last point, namely the limitations of psychological explanations of behavior. In social systems there are a large number of constraints upon the range of alternatives available to any particular individual. Some of these constraints arise from biological and environmental aspects of the human condition. Other constraints stem from the given level of technology available for manipulating either the external environment of a person or his own biological system.

Perhaps more important is the extent to which the psychological experience of a person is constrained by social processes. The inputs of experience to an individual are mediated by psychological processes, but the content of the experience varies according to social situations. Within any society there are quite different kinds of social situations. These are not randomly distributed over the society, and are not shared by all individuals. We must attempt to comprehend the influence of social variables upon these social situations and therefore on the distribution of the content of psychological experiences within a society. In this way we shall conceive of the subjective biases of individuals as in part resulting from social processes.

We must develop a procedure for constructing our theories that enables us to consider the widest possible range of variables as candidates for inclusion in our equations. But we must also adhere to our several strict criteria for admission.

We shall state the theoretical influence of our variables directly upon the set of individuals in the society—for example, the variables and outcomes are defined over individuals. We shall ask, given an individual of specific characteristics (including the history of acquiring the characteristics), can we predict the outcome for him in the next time period? If we could predict for all individuals then we could predict for the total population by adding. Unfortunately, our knowledge of what an individual is likely to do in the future can come only from our study of what similar individuals have done in the past. Thus we are committed to the study of sets of individuals. We shall attempt to estimate the probability that a particular outcome will occur to a given set of individuals. As a convenience in stating our theory we shall use metaphors that refer to a hypothetical individual.

Our hypothetical individual has characteristics that will vary over time. This variation will depend partly on characteristics in the history of the given individual—his age, for example—and partly on characteristic events in the history of his society, such as wars and depressions. These two kinds of time must be represented differently; ordinarily we will use age in years at last birthday for the individual and calendar years for the society. In order to keep this distinction clear we shall express our theory in terms of predictions for a particular hypothetical age cohort—that is, a set of individuals of the same age in the same calendar year. Thus the consequences of age will be uniform within the cohort. In addition, our form of theoretical statement will follow a particular hypothetical cohort from birth to death, thus expressing the consequences of age. The consequences of historical events such as wars and depressions will be spelled out hypothetically for every age of the hypothetical cohort. Thus we must define the complete set of hypothetical conditional probabilities for each age and for each calendar year.

If we proceed in this way the aggregation of our theory to the total society will consist of taking each of the successive age cohorts, modifying the predictions for the different ages at which calendar-year events occur in each age cohort, and then obtaining predictions over all ages within any given calendar year. Such predictions are relatively easy to test with empirical data—for example, census data.

We must express the outcomes for individuals and their age cohorts as conditional upon social variables. Within age cohorts we wish to differentiate these social variables, while in successive cohorts we wish to keep track of the history of the individuals with respect to these variables. To see the kind of difficulties that arise in this problem one should recall the discussion in Chapter 1 of births as dependent upon the area of mother. These procedures allow us to regard social change as stemming from changes in individuals, from differences in successive age cohorts, or from general social events.

It will be convenient to approximate the language of economics and of psychology in the decision theory that we shall use. But we shall also have to modify the meanings and extend the vocabulary in order to deal with the particular prediction problems that we have chosen in this book. These meanings will gain empirical clarity as we proceed with the next few chapters.

Our decision theory must be stated so that psychological and social variables can both be represented as parameters upon which the outcome depends. We shall attempt to do this with several devices, some of which have already been introduced above.

In order to incorporate these social variables in our

theoretical statement we shall use metaphors from decision theory. Thus we shall speak of an individual making a selection among a given set of alternatives when we wish to predict the outcome for him. We shall have to predict the set of alternatives that are available to the individual as well as the criteria used by the individual in making the selection. This is the "subjective" aspect of the prediction problem mentioned above.

We shall assume, for a hypothetical individual, that a behavioral outcome is a result of the selection of alternatives by him. Further, we shall assume that the individual selects alternatives in terms of the consequences that he ascribes to them.

Note that we are not attempting to predict the conscious content of the individual's mind accompanying his selection of alternatives. We want to predict the outcome of the decision process, the overt behavior. Thus the decision metaphors are used to obtain a reasonable set of equations.

The alternatives and the consequences are assumed to be perceived by the individual to some degree. We shall further assume that this perception may vary widely over a population of individuals. The process of selection will also vary. This is the subjective aspect of the problem outlined above.

The classic discussion of this problem assumes that the complete set of alternatives is known to the decision maker and that he is able to assign a pair of numbers to each alternative. One number is the probability of the occurrence of the alternative, often called the *likelihood of the alternative*; the other number indexes the desirability of the alternative, and is often called the *utility of the alternative*. According to the classic discussion, decision making takes place in the following way: The individual takes the product of the pair of numbers associated with each alternative, compares the resulting products for all alternatives, and selects that alternative with the largest product, thus maximizing his expected utility.[1]

The classic discussion was developed primarily in order to improve decision making, not to explain it. Efforts to bend the classic discussion to the prediction of actual behavior are relatively recent and, for the most part, deal with behavior in small groups that are experimentally contrived.[2] We wish to predict to very large aggregates of persons in situations that we cannot experimentally control. Therefore we must beware of blindly borrowing aspects of the classic discussion.

One aspect of the classic discussion that has been controversial in recent years is the decision rule, namely maximum expected utility. Other mathematical rules for selecting alternatives in terms of likelihoods and utilities have been proposed—for example, minimizing the maximum risk. These rules, however, do not, for the most part, meet our objections to the classic discussion, namely its insufficiency for predicting change. They were developed for the case of uncertainty in the subjective estimates either of utilities or of likelihoods.

We need to know how the decision process for an individual varies with time. Are the number and spacing of births set once and for all at an early age, or are they tentative, subject to later revision? The latter alternative, which seems more reasonable, commits us to sequential decision making.

In sequential decision making we assume that the individual can reestimate the probabilities of alternatives and the utilities of alternatives at successive points in time. If the new estimates differ sufficiently from the old, then it is possible that a different alternative may be selected. The decision rule governing the selection of alternatives in the light of new estimates need not be identical with the decision rule that previously or initially governed selection for an individual. Perhaps initial selection approximates the maximum expected utility rule, whereas subsequent selection follows a rule that gives additional weight to the alternative initially selected. The "satisficing" rule proposed by Herbert A. Simon is an example of a rule that gives greater weight to the initial alternative in subsequent selection by giving less weight to increases in the maximum expected utility of the alternatives initially rejected.[3] Thus the decision rule itself can be treated as a variable that we attempt to predict. Sequential decision making is compatible with a cohort representation of social systems.

The process of sequential reestimation must take account of the variables that can influence the estimates. We can assume that an individual is an information processor, is constantly receiving new information from the "environment," and can reevaluate his choice of alternatives with this information. We must specify an equation or equations that contain "information" variables as parameters and yield likelihoods and utilities as dependent variables. Such equations now become the focus of our attention.

It is important to describe the future time perspective of our individual in these equations. Some individuals will consider only short-run "rewards," whereas others may concentrate on long-run rewards. New information might imply a decrease in the short-run reward and an increase in the long-run reward from the same alternative. Unless we specify how our individual weighs short-run against long-run reward, we cannot predict his choice.

The future time perspective also enters into the estimates of likelihoods. Is it the probability of occurrence in the short run or the long run that is being estimated? Unless we know we will have no rule to tell us how new information modifies the decision process. If we did not care about social change this would not matter, but since we do care about social change it matters a great deal.

Suppose we assume that the individual estimates the total utility over a period of time (the integral of a utility curve with respect to time). The limits of integration and the shape of the curve are then allowed to vary among individuals and for the same individual over time. The estimation of likelihoods can be viewed in the same way. For an example from fertility, note that Banks' theory implies lifetime budgeting on the part of the upper middle classes, especially in the estimation of the total educational cost of children. Thus they estimate income and expenditure curves over the period of dependency of children, perhaps as long as thirty years. Note further that Banks' theory assumes a readjustment of utilities as new information, say a depression, yields new estimates of total utility.

We can also illustrate the reestimation of likelihoods from fertility. The diffusion of new technology makes new alternatives available to the individuals, and thus alters the likelihoods of the alternatives available to the individual. (In any particular research problem a set of alternatives can be defined by the investigator which include the relevant possibilities; if an individual is completely unaware of a possibility then a subjective likelihood of zero could be assigned in his case. Note, however, that this procedure does not distinguish between ignorance of an alternative and the estimation of a zero likelihood for an alternative.) The invention and diffusion of new techniques of birth control change the available alternatives which can influence individual fertility rates.

Suppose we have equations that predict sequential decisions contingent upon new estimates of the consequences of alternatives. In these equations we will have behavior as outputs and information as inputs to the decision maker. Now we must develop a new equation, or set of equations, that gives us information as an output, or dependent variable.

In general it is quite difficult to specify such new information. However, there is one approach. We can study the differential patterns of communication in society. The distribution of contacts among persons in a society follows certain regularities. Thus we would expect that, given a new innovation and its starting point in a society, we can predict the pattern of its diffusion.

The flow of information may modify likelihoods and utilities. However, these two possibilities may occur in different ways. In general the utilities are regarded as more stable and resistant to change. Such preferences are deeply imbedded in the emotional structure of an individual; they are formed in close personal relationships with others, perhaps in early childhood. Psychologists ordinarily discuss these stabilities as aspects of attitudes, in which cognitive (likelihood) and emotional (utility) elements become embedded together in a particular psychological configuration.

If, for a given decision, the individual's accounting system is essentially instrumental or pragmatic, then the reestimates of likelihoods may be relatively independent of the individual's stable emotional structure, and thus he may adjust with relative rapidity to new information. If the decision is not an instrumental type but has become embedded in the emotional structure of the individual then new information will be ignored. Thus the decision rule depends in part on the emotional structure of the individual. The possibilities for change in the emotional structure depend greatly upon the past and present close personal relationships of an individual.

The distribution of close personal relationships in a society is far more predictable than the distribution of all contacts that a person may have. Knowledge of this distribution is our greatest single asset in the prediction problem we have set for ourselves. In order to predict the distribution of close personal contacts in a society we turn to segregation theory. Elsewhere I have argued that this distribution is well indexed by the distribution of the marriages within a society.[4] If the probability of inter-marriage between any two sets of persons is relatively high, then the probability of close personal contacts and relationships between them is also relatively high.

Thus if we wish to predict changes in utilities we must turn to a study of close personal relationships. These relationships are important for defining communication channels. We still must predict the content of the communication through the channels. Here the sociological discussion of values is helpful.

Let us illustrate again with fertility. We have two problems. First is the prediction of the diffusion of birth-control technology throughout a society. Second is the prediction of the fertility behavior of the users of the new technology.

As previously noted, the diffusion of technology meets boundaries imposed by the prior distribution of utilities, say the religious effect. The fertility behavior of planners also illustrates the influence of the distribution of utilities —for example, the ideal family size. How about the change in utilities?

Here we see a need to keep track of the communication of values (utilities) across generations as well as within generations. To what extent are ideal family-size preferences derived from one's own parents, as opposed to the extent that they come from one's peers? Given an answer to this question, we still must determine the content of the values communicated from parents and from peers.

The content of the values communicated can best be estimated with direct social-psychological measurements. These measurements must establish the distribution of values, the flow of values, and the stability of values within the system. Given the results of social-psychological measurements, we can then deduce the behavioral consequences of such values and test with census and vital-statistics data. Lacking such social-psychological measurements we must supply the relevant parameters by crude hypothesis and indirect procedures—such as the methods of Banks.

In the next chapter we shall attempt to combine the argument of Banks with the results of social-psychological measurements made to date. In so doing we shall have to stay close to U.S. data, as most of the social-psychological research has been carried out here.

Let us now shift from a hypothetical individual-planning fertility to a hypothetical family-planning fertility. The family plan emerges from the values (utilities) of husband and wife. Thus we must have a theory that enables us to deduce the family plan given the characteristics of husband and wife. The relevant characteristics will enable us to define the relationship between husband and wife as well as the values of each individual.

When we focus on the family we raise the question of "joint decision making." This question is dealt with in small-group social psychology and in organization theory. Small-group social psychology emphasizes communication within a group, whereas organization theory attempts to define relationships within a group. Efforts to combine the two types of theory are seen in works by March and Simon[5] and Thibaut and Kelley.[6] For our purposes we need only note that the relationships within a group may be defined as the parameters in an equation that produces the communication processes as an output.

A crucial issue in joint decision making is the partitioning of the decision among the participants. This partitioning can be defined in terms of relationships or in terms of communication. In this book we shall argue that the partitioning of the fertility decision in the middle-class American family is different from the partitioning of the migration decision for the same family. Thus we argue that the fertility joint decision is the result of a mutual discussion and agreement on the range of issues by both—an essentially egalitarian or "voting" decision; whereas the migration decision depends upon two forms of specialized knowledge possessed separately by husband and wife—one concerned with the husband's job and the other with the household.

Now let us review the social variables. They have been introduced as indices of the contact networks throughout society and thus as indices of the diffusion of technology and of communication throughout society. As such they constrain the communication of information that influences the subjective estimation of likelihoods and of utilities on the part of the individuals in the society.

In Chapter 2 we saw that religion and politics also influenced fertility behavior. In effect they set boundaries on the diffusion and communication processes. These boundaries are to some degree permeable. In the matter of religion, the members may leave, or the organization may change its position abruptly, or there may be a slow change of the behavior of members. Thus the religious effect may be more like friction that slows diffusion than a boundary that stops diffusion. In the matter of political systems there are the possibilities of revolution or of change of position (a thaw). Here the sanctions that can be brought to bear are often more severe than the religious sanctions (unless religion and politics are coterminous), and thus a less permeable boundary is possible.

The important factor for us is the influence of religious and political variables in the context of the breakdown of traditional society. To bring out this factor we must first consider the implications of the notion of traditional society for the psychological theory that we have discussed above. The decision rules of individuals may change during the breakdown of traditional society. The variables and equations that define the relevance of new information may also change.

Characteristic patterns of decision making differ vastly between traditional and modern societies. In order to describe the differences Weber used the notion of modes of orientation. The modes of orientation that interest us are slightly modified from the ones Weber used. We shall describe three modes—traditional, short-run hedonistic, and purposive-rational. The first is the same as that of Weber, the second roughly parallels Weber's affectual mode, and the third combines the *Wertrational* and *Zweckrational* modes of Weber.[7]

From a decision viewpoint a crucial difference among the modes of orientation is the future time perspective. The traditional mode of orientation implies no crystallized future time perspective for an individual. There is no sequential decision making. The individual acting in the traditional mode selects the same alternative that he selected before with no recourse to new information.

He follows custom. Thus prediction of his behavior is made by studying the customs and the culture, not by examining his psychological characteristics.

The individual acting in the short-run hedonistic mode has a very brief future time perspective. The calculation of likelihoods and of utilities takes account of a brief time period in the future. In order to predict the behavior of a person acting in the short-run hedonistic mode we would need to estimate highly evanescent situational factors that influence the person directly—the immediate psychological situation in which the person finds himself.

The individual acting in the purposive-rational mode has an elaborate time perspective extending far into the future. His calculation of likelihoods and of utilities is complex and intricate, and is very sensitive to new information. The argument of Banks on fertility clearly assumes such a mode of orientation.

From a macro perspective the three orientations differ in regard to sanctions, or punishments. The traditional mode is closely bound to a system of sanctions that govern the behavior of the individual. In particular, the ubiquity of punishments for deviation characterizes the society in which we find the traditional mode widespread. If we wish to predict change then we should study the agencies or organizations that dispense the sanctions—religious, political, military, etc.

In the short-run hedonistic mode official sanctions have lost their monolithic and rigid appearance to the individual. Outside of the immediate situation, sanctions have an unpredictable, perhaps random, appearance to the individual.

In the purposive-rational mode the sanctions are predictable, and indeed are taken into account by the individual when he estimates his own utilities. Each individual can revise his selection of alternatives if he believes that sanctions have changed.

It should be clear that the individual with a purposive-rational mode of orientation is a sequential decision maker. From a purely mathematical perspective we could regard each of the other modes of orientation as special cases of sequential decision making, or of the purposive-rational mode. But as variables they are important special cases to which we must be able to refer when we make models of the breakdown of traditional society.

Briefly, we may regard the feudal society of the West as a political, religious, and military equilibrium in which most of the population—peasants in particular—was held in check by crude punishments. As technology, commerce, urbanization, and the like modified the feudal society, the purposive-rational mode of orientation appeared among the urban upper middle classes, especially the salaried professionals (according to Weber a by-product of the Protestant Reformation). But the peasants and urban lower classes experienced such great disruption from the decline of feudal society that the short run hedonistic mode of orientation became more characteristic. These latter groups take on the purposive-rational mode of orientation when: (1) there is a relatively long-term stability of the social system that enables them to get their bearings, and (2) there is a sufficiently great contact with the previous urban middle classes that the appropriate attitudes can diffuse through interpersonal relationships to the newcomer groups.

The illustration of these notions with fertility is found in the demographic transition. The high fertility in the first stage is a consequence of a set of customs which are adhered to by persons acting in the traditional mode of orientation. The innovators who adopt family planning are persons acting in the purposive-rational mode. The diffusion of family planning is limited to the persons in the population acting in the purposive-rational mode. Those in the traditional mode or in the short-run hedonistic mode cannot acquire these practices; however, persons are capable of changing modes. The fertility behavior of planners is represented by the purposive-rational mode—that is, by equations that represent sequential decision making of a highly calculating type.

NOTES

1. Herman Chernoff and Lincoln E. Moses, *Elementary Decision Theory* (New York: Wiley, 1959); R. Duncan Luce and Howard Raiffa, *Games and Decisions* (New York: Wiley, 1958); John von Neumann and Oskar Morgenstern, *Theory of Games and Economic Behavior*, 3rd ed. (Princeton, N.J.: Princeton U. P., 1953); Abraham Wald, *Statistical Decision Functions* (New York: Wiley, 1956).

2. Sidney Siegel and Lawrence E. Fouraker, *Bargaining and Group Decision Making* (New York: McGraw-Hill, 1960); J. W. Thibaut and H. H. Kelley, *The Social Psychology of Groups* (New York: Wiley, 1959).

3. Herbert A. Simon, "Theories of Decision Making in Economics and Behavioral Science," *American Economic Review*, XLIX (June 1959), 253–83.

4. James M. Beshers, *Urban Social Structure* (New York: Free Press, 1962).

5. J. G. March and H. A. Simon, *Organizations* (New York: Wiley, 1959).

6. Thibaut and Kelley, *op. cit.*

7. Max Weber, *The Theory of Social and Economic Organization*, trans. by Talcott Parsons (New York: Free Press, 1947).

CHAPTER 4

Fertility

IN this chapter we will review the findings of social
psychological studies of fertility. Two studies will
receive major attention, the Indianapolis study[1] and
the study of Puerto Rican fertility by Hill, Stycos, and
Back.[2] Other results will be examined in the light of the
apparent implications of these studies.

We do not wish to examine all aspects of these
studies, but rather to focus on their relation to the theoretical discussion in Chapter 3. Therefore we might well
summarize the theoretical issues at the outset.

We have sketched out a theory of sequential decision
making subject to social constraints. There are three
types of social constraints on decision processes that bear
on the decline of births in the West. First is the Weberian

constraint of mode of orientation, the extent to which the person calculates the long-range consequences of the alternatives and selects alternatives accordingly. Second is the Banks hypothesis that the calculation of the future status of children enters into budget construction and yields the desired pattern of births among persons that plan in the sense of Weber's purposive-rational mode of orientation. Since Banks' hypothesis presupposes Weber's hypothesis, we shall sometimes refer to the pair as the Weber-Banks hypothesis. The third constraint derives from consideration of the family as a two-person decision unit; the agreement on goals and the implementation of these goals through appropriate use of birth-control methods are dependent upon the effectiveness of family decision processes, the degree of dependence varying with the characteristics of the method of birth control (with sterilization perhaps the least dependent). Thus the prediction of fertility patterns from these decision-process theories is conditional upon the social constraints plus the distribution of methods of birth control.

In order to compare these theories with research on families we must specify the methods of birth control known, the existence of long-range plans, the goals of these plans specified in desired numbers and spacing of children, and the characteristics of the decision process by which the couple implements the plan. Further, we should specify the time trend in these characteristics of families—in particular, the previous diffusion process that might have led to the present distribution of characteristics by families.

With the Indianapolis study we can for the first time separate out these three aspects of family planning and investigate each. The main limitations for our purposes stem from the characteristics of the sample used in the study. Because the interviews were conducted in 1941 an undue weight upon the economic parameters of the 1930's is found in the data. Further homogeneity of the data results from the exclusion of nonwhites, Catholics, Jews, and the foreign-born from the sample. Thus the system response to changing social parameters is restricted in this sample, as well as the differentiation of this response. Indeed, the sample almost entirely excludes the rural population as well as the cases listed above. Our ability to test the diffusion of Weberian modes of orientation is severely hampered by the homogeneity of the sample.

The other shortcomings of the Indianapolis study stem from its atheoretical character, but we resolve that difficulty here by supplying our own theory.

The findings of the Indianapolis study were published in various papers scattered over more than a decade, with different authors supplying different perspectives to the publications. One summary article, however, was authored by the senior research staff.[3] We shall concentrate our attention on this article.

A highly convenient summary table is provided in the article. In this table the many measurements, social and psychological, obtained in the household survey are organized into twenty-three variables. Each of these twenty-three variables is contained in two hypotheses: (1) that this variable is correlated with planning (use of birth control to achieve at least one planned pregnancy), and (2) that this variable is correlated with family-size objectives of planners (but here results are reported only for those couples who planned all pregnancies). The twenty-three variables are further grouped into five major categories.

The hypothesis of correlation with planning implies

Table 4-1 — Summary of Indianapolis study findings*

CLASS AND SUBJECT OF HYPOTHESIS	DIRECTION OF RELATION FOUND		HAS THE HYPOTHESIS BEEN SUPPORTED?	
	Fertility-Planning Status	Size of Completely Planned Family	Fertility-Planning Status	Size of Completely Planned Family
I. Status and Security				
Socioeconomic status	+	+	Yes	No
Economic insecurity	−	−	No	Yes
Economic tension	−	+	No[1]	No[1]
II. Community and Family Background				
Family and childhood situations	±	±	Partially	Partially
Residence and migration history	±	±	Partially	Partially
Doubling-up of families Health of wife and husband	+	−	No[2]	No[2]
Health of children	+	−	No[2]	No[2]
III. Interest in Home and Children				
Liking for children	0	+	No	Partially
Parental preference regarding sex of children	DNA	±	DNA	Partially
Children wanting brothers and sisters	DNA	+	DNA	Partially
Reasons for Second Child:				
Belief "only child" handicapped	DNA	+	DNA	Partially
Desire to insure against childlessness	DNA	+	DNA	Partially
IV. Personality Characteristics				
Personal inadequacy	−	−	No	Partially
Feeling children interfere with personal freedom	−	+	No	No
Ego-centered interest in children	+	−	Partially	Partially
Fear of pregnancy	+	−	Partially	Partially
Rationality of Behavior				
Tendency to plan	+	−	Partially	Partially
Interest in religion	−	+	Partially	Partially
Adherence to traditions	−	+	Partially	Partially
Conformity to group patterns	±	±	Partially	Partially
V. Marital Adjustment and Husband-Wife Dominance				
Marital adjustment	+	+	Yes	Partially
Husband-wife dominance	0	0	No[3]	No[3]

+ = Direct relation with hypothesis variable.
− = Inverse relation with hypothesis variable.
0 = No relation with hypothesis variable.
DNA = Does not apply.

[1] Results believed to be spurious because of selective factors.
[2] Data on health very inadequate.
[3] Some results found on reformulated hypothesis.
* Pascal K. Whelpton and Clyde V. Kiser (eds.) *Social and Psychological Factors Affecting Fertility,* Vol. 5 (New York: Milbank Memorial Fund, 1958), pp. 1332–1333.

two kinds of diffusion processes throughout a society—diffusion of birth-control technology and diffusion of "planning" attitudes of the sort that we have identified with the purposive-rational mode of orientation in Weberian sociology. The Weberian argument, however, is applicable to those persons who have planned every pregnancy, not to those who have planned only the most recent pregnancy; for the purposive-rational mode of orientation is supposed to be a personality characteristic acquired prior to maturity, and therefore prior to marriage. Those persons who turned to birth control after having one or more children would seem to be making a short-run situational adjustment rather than a carefully calculated one.

Within the group that planned every pregnancy we might expect Banks' argument to hold. Thus the hypothesis on number of children should reflect the behavior of parents maximizing the status of their children within the constraints of career-income curves. The plans to space children might also reflect the parents' computation of the costs of college education.

The success of planning, the achievement of goals, is related to the characteristics of the two-person decision process. We shall consider this point with reference to the two variables termed marital adjustment and husband-wife dominance.

Let us now examine the table to determine which of the forty-six hypotheses held by the research team are supported. We find only three clear-cut cases of support. Let us discuss these cases first, then turn to the various clouds that were cast over the other forty-three hypotheses.

Two of the three hypotheses that emerge unscathed have to do with the influence of economic and social position. The first is that planning itself has a significant negative correlation with socioeconomic status. Within the group of persons who completely planned their families, however, we find that number of children has a positive correlation with economic position. The second finding was not expected by the research team, but the pair of findings is precisely what one would predict from Banks' theory—namely, that diffusion of planning is downward from the salaried professionals, and that planners adjust their fertility in order to protect the social status of their children within the constraints set by their career income. Since the basic cost of this goal is the college education, planners, budgets are set off from nonplanners, budgets by this minimum lump per child, but since there is a ceiling upon such educational costs, additional income makes possible additional children.

The other economic hypothesis that was supported was that economic insecurity was negatively correlated with fertility within the group of completely planned families (again Banks) but the research team was surprised to learn that economic insecurity was also negatively correlated with planning, that the most economically insecure did not plan. (But it turned out that, in the total population, lower-income people realistically had greater insecurity about income than higher-income people.) The latter finding fits with the Weber-Banks hypothesis that planning as a mode of orientation diffuses downward, but has not yet reached the bottom, perhaps because economic insecurity generates a short-run mode of response that is inconsistent with planning.

The other two economic hypotheses failed; they were correlations between fertility and economic tension (defined as discrepancy between actual and desired standard of living). The researchers found that large discrepancies in standard of living were associated with larger numbers of children. They explained away this result with the observation that, in the general population, large discrepancies are associated with low incomes; but within the completely planned families this line of thought will not work, because larger numbers of children were associated with higher income. From the point of view of Banks the measures of discrepancy of standard of living used are irrelevant, as no effort was made to measure desired standard of living for children. Banks' argument turns on the discrepancy between the sum of standard of living for self plus standard of living for children on the one hand and the career income on the other.

Since the Weber-Banks theory seems so reasonable at this point it is interesting to note why the research team rejects such a theory. There are three grounds. First, they found that planning was correlated with a rationality factor of the type that one might expect from Weber, but when they found that rationality was also highly associated with socioeconomic status, they viewed the association of rationality with planning as a consequence of the association of socioeconomic status with planning. They did not see that Banks' theory predicts that all three correlations among rationality, socioeconomic status, and planning are high when only 40 per cent plan. Of course, if planning diffuses throughout all the population, the correlation of socioeconomic status with planning vanishes.

Second, the questions on parents' attitudes toward children were not relevant. Although the research team made a great effort to establish liking of children as an important variable, it did not perform well when empirically tested. If, however, they had related liking for children to the aspirations and plans for children, then this variable could have been introduced into a Banks' type of hypothesis.

Third, the relevant data on social mobility were interpreted without reference to a Weber-Banks hypothesis. Note that "the planned families of socially mobile couples are smaller than the planned families of socially non-mobile couples of comparable status;" but "upwardly mobile couples . . . [held] . . . a position intermediate in fertility planning effectiveness between the levels of effectiveness of origin and destination groups."[4] This finding supports the idea of downward diffusion of a compulsive personality type, the purposive-rational mode of orientation.

The other interesting findings of the study have to do with the success of couples in achieving goals. Thus the positive correlation of marital adjustment with planning (the third hypothesis that was supported) turns out to be less interesting than the fact that marital adjustment is positively correlated with success among planners. In addition, we find that if husband and wife agree that decision making is "fifty-fifty" between them, then, among planners, success is greater. Finally, if persons evidence self-confidence and feelings of personal adequacy then, among planners, success is greater. Thus the two-person decision process is relevant to fertility theory.

In summary, from our present perspective the Indianapolis study offers strong support for the Weber-Banks hypothesis and for the theory of the family as a two-person decision unit in fertility planning. The relationships of socioeconomic status with planning, given a population of 40 per cent planners, were substantiated in a manner that closely parallels the diffusion argument that Banks developed for Victorian England.

The Puerto Rican study, *The Family and Population Control*, was developed out of the experience of the

Indianapolis study. The research team, however, emphasized sociology and group social psychology in its senior
staff, in contrast with the emphasis upon demography
and individual psychology in the Indianapolis study.
Further, a basic obligation to one of the sponsors, the
Puerto Rican government, was to discover relationships
between fertility and social factors that could lead to
methods for controlling fertility.

In a previous Puerto Rican study Paul Hatt had amply
demonstrated that the correlations of fertility and socioeconomic status were similar to those found in Indianapolis.[5] However, such relations were little guide to policy
makers for they implied, if anything, that an improved
standard of living should be the appropriate target of the
government in a fertility-reduction program. This was not
helpful, as the purpose of the fertility-reduction program
itself was to increase the standard of living. Further, a
Weber-Banks theory would not imply that an increased
standard of living would lead to decreased fertility unless
new modes of orientation and new social-status objectives
were introduced as well.

In order to detect variables that might be modified by
an action program, the research team chose to concentrate on family decision-making processes in the lower
class. They organized their research into three stages:
exploratory, quantitative verification, and experimental
validation. The first stage was directed toward specifica-
tion of the relevant variables and the development of
appropriate measurement techniques. Thus anthropologi-
cal field observation and open-ended interviewing were
the main research techniques. The second stage was devoted to verification with interviews of lower-class clients
of public-health clinics. The third stage consisted of an

evaluation of experimental action programs, an effort to contrast the effectiveness of several different methods of introducing family planning into rural villages.

First we shall review the results of the verification survey. This survey resembles the Indianapolis study but had important differences. The restriction of the sample to lower class respondents greatly reduced the influence of measures of socioeconomic status upon planning and upon fertility. The social-psychological variables were explicitly related to all other variables in the survey, thus permitting the statement of hypotheses that were, in the main, supported.

The survey results do not throw much further light on the Weber-Banks hypothesis. We note that the sample was heavily weighted toward the lower class. From the Weber-Banks hypothesis we would not expect diffusion of planning to this class until after it was well established in the upper middle classes and middle classes; in fact, traces of long-term and regular use of birth control appear here only in the youngest, most urban, best educated, and most upwardly mobile persons in the sample (as we might expect), even though knowledge of and use of birth-control methods were widespread. That the compulsive personality associated with the purposive-rational mode of orientation is rare is further suggested by the great gap between the expressed preferred family sizes and the actual family sizes. Despite sporadic use of birth control there is an undesired excess in family size.

We note also that practically no one in the sample used birth control before the first pregnancy, few before the third pregnancy. Thus the spacing to achieve budget control that the Weber-Banks hypothesis implies is not apparent.

Figure 4–1

A FACTOR ANALYTIC MODEL OF FERTILITY DYNAMICS

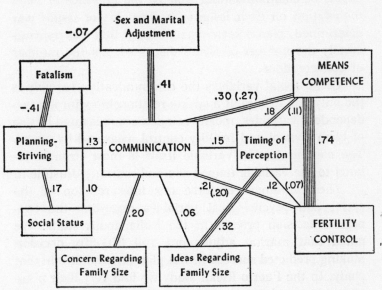

CODE: (1) Figures in parentheses are partial correlations, holding all other factors constant. All other figures are zero-order correlation coefficients.

(2) The size of the correlation coefficient is approximated by the number of lines between factors; correlations less than 0.10 are not statistically significant at the 5 percent level.

Source: Reuben Hill, J. Mayone Stycos, and Kurt W. Back, *The Family and Population Control* (Chapel Hill, U. of North Carolina Press, 1959), Figure 7, p. 246.

The survey results on the family-decision process are best seen in the light of the measures of communication between husband and wife. Let us look at the diagram (Figure 4-1) summarizing the network of intercorrelations. The box labeled communication has a central position in the network (as revealed by factor analysis). (As a graduate student I carried out the bulk of the computations reported here; thus I am responsible for both computational errors and interpretational errors in what follows.) The communication variable is measured as the extent of communication; that is, the presence of communication on each issue of a given list of issues was determined, then a score was assigned that was approximately the number of issues discussed, not the number of conversations.

Of all social variables the communication variable is the only one to exhibit a strong relationship with the two dependent variables, means competence measured by use of birth control and fertility control measured by births. The communication variable itself is most strongly related to the variable named sex and marital adjustment.

These findings reinforce our interpretation of the social and psychological variables regarding the two-person decision process in the Indianapolis study. We noted that marital adjustment and fifty-fifty decision making predicted success within planning families in that study. In the Puerto Rican study we find very little planning compared to the Indianapolis study (less than 5 per cent planned every birth compared to more than 40 per cent), yet we find a relationship between effectiveness of planning and communication in Puerto Rico.

If communication is correlated with successful planning we still need to know whether an increase in communication by an action program will yield more successful planning. This question was put to test in the experimental phase of the project. The answer is yes. A purely medical discussion of birth control in villages resulted in numerous trials, but these were discontinued within a year. When the medical discussion was supplemented by a special educational program aimed at increasing the communication between husband and wife —and therefore the joint decision-making capacity of the couple, a significant percentage of the birth-control users continued regular and effective use.

It is relevant to conjecture that the egalitarian character of the two-person decision process is itself a product of Westernization which accompanies the diffusion of the purposive-rational mode of orientation, but is not identical to it. Certainly Weber's discussions of bureaucracy as a form of social organization seem to imply such a conjecture. The discovery that communication can be altered by relatively modest action programs is, however, not implied by Weber.

A number of recent American studies deserve comment. Before we can interpret these recent studies we must extend our theory to account for fertility differences between religions, races, social classes, and rural and urban residents at any given time. Until now we have considered differences among social classes as a result of diffusion processes that originate in the upper middle classes. The diffusion processes are also assumed to account for the urban and rural differences in fertility. We have to consider the extent to which this argument can be generalized for religious, racial, and other social distinctions.

Note that the several diffusion processes are somewhat different in character; they need not always occur together, and certainly need not be perfectly correlated. The diffusion of modes of orientation and the diffusion of birth-control technology seemed to be quite different in the Puerto Rican study. The diffusion of particular family-size ideals and of fifty-fifty decision making in a family might also follow different patterns, or, at least, different time lags.

The prediction that we seek to make for each such diffusion process is the point at which it enters a society, the rate at which it spreads through the society, the existence of partial boundaries to the spread which might change the rate of spread, and the existence of complete boundaries across which there is no spread. We would like to predict the order of segments of society in which diffusion occurs, and we would like to predict the rate of diffusion within each segment. Our predictions as to the resulting pattern of differential fertility at any given time period can then be determined.

The issue now turns on the presence of boundaries in social diffusion. We have two problems: (1) Are different kinds of boundaries relevant to the diffusion of different kinds of social objects? (2) For any given type of social object, are there several different kinds of boundaries to diffusion? Let us state a theory of social diffusion over all objects and boundaries, then consider the qualifications that must be made for special cases.

The common theories of social diffusion include the following three points: (1) Social diffusion follows communication links in a society; (2) The more personal the communication link the more likely the diffusion; and (3) The more prestigeful the source of diffusion the more likely the diffusion. The first point includes mass media of communication as well as personal communication. The second point is a qualification of the first point which holds for differential social objects—i.e., the more deeply the object is embedded in the personality of the individual, the greater the significance of personal contacts in diffusion, especially the close emotional contacts. The third point stresses imitation in status seeking, but insofar as different segments of society assign prestige in the same way, diffusion will resemble the flow of fashion; yet if some segments of society reject the prestige order of the larger society, a boundary to diffusion is created.

Roughly speaking, we expect social diffusion to follow the distribution of personal contacts in a society, especially those contacts that symbolize equality between persons. We expect that measures of segregation, in particular the probability of intermarriage, will best index the patterns of social diffusion from one segment of society to another. Let us see how this view holds up for particular diffusion processes.

First, we have to consider the diffusion of a "planning" or "purposive-rational" mode of orientation. Budgeting of time and money and compulsiveness of behavior appear after the breakdown of the traditional society and its associated traditional mode of orientation. It was Max Weber's contention that the origin of such behavior was partly determined by cultural conditions—specifically, the religious-belief system. Given the appearance of such behavior in the West, we still have to determine the preconditions for its diffusion. What factors influence the rate of diffusion of modes of orientation? How do we explain the fact that the urban middle classes seem always to be the first planners on a society? Is there an intermediate period of cultural disorganization in the transitions in which a "short-run hedonistic" mode of orientation is commonplace, as in Albert Cohen's analysis of the urban lower classes?[6]

Second, given that the planning mode of orientation has diffused to some persons, we must study the diffusion of birth-control technology to those persons. This problem can be approached in a manner parallel to the study of the acceptance of technological change by other social scientists. Specific information and specific items of technology may be traced and their rates of flow estimated, as has been done by rural sociologists in the study of technological change in agriculture.

Third, we must consider the diffusion of specific values, namely ideal family-size values, to those families which practice planning. There is every reason to expect fluctuations in the ideal family size, due either to general changes in economic and social conditions, or changes specific to particular families. A decision mechanism will be necessary to express such fluctuations. But note that a two-person decision process is involved, thus requiring that the decision theory be embedded in a group-theory context. Technological developments in birth control (e.g., "the pill") might reduce the decision process to one person in the future, but we shall have to await this development.

We can summarize these remarks in Table 4-2. Time passes from left to right.

In the table the modes of orientation are characteristics of individuals that typify their orientations toward a large number of activities and social objects. Thus it is possible for a person to have a traditional mode of orientation, in general, but to deviate with respect to fertility. We assume that such deviations in the orientation toward fertility from the general mode of orientation is a rare case.

It is possible to characterize societies, or segments of societies, by the mode of orientation most common to the persons in the society. In this way we can represent the demographic transition of societies as a movement from the upper left-hand corner (cells 1 and 2) to the lower right-hand corner (cells 11 and 12). There is no necessary path of transition through the intervening cells. Neither persons nor societies need pass through the short-run hedonistic mode, nor is it certain that knowledge of birth-control devices comes after the transition to a

Table 4-2 — Diffusion processes schematized

MODES OF ORIENTATION

		Traditional	Short-run Hedonistic	Purposive-Rational
		(1)	(5)	(9)
No knowledge of modern birth control methods	High ideal family size	Typical peasant village	Jamaica? high illegitimacy unstable families venereal disease?	Rare case but same as (1)
		(2)	(6)	(10)
	Low ideal family size	Delayed marriage infanticide? coitus interruptus rhythm	Distinction from (5) not possible as unstable family inhibits joint decision process	Rare case but same as (2)
		(3)	(7)	(11)
Knowledge of modern birth control methods	High ideal family size	Rare case B.C. not used	B.C. not used	Current U.S.?
		(4)	(8)	(12)
	Low ideal family size	Rare case B.C. not used with regularity	B.C. not used with regularity	Current Western Europe

purposive-rational mode of orientation, though this apparently occurred in the West.

We must now specify the mechanisms of diffusion that are involved in these three cases. The first case, the diffusion of modes of orientation, is the most complex and least understood. The major mechanism of diffusion of the purposive-rational mode of orientation is sustained close personal relationships, as in the childhood socialization process. To the extent that both the traditional and the purposive-rational modes of orientation both emphasize the development of personal constraint, it is possible for an adult to move from the former to the latter as a result of relatively casual contacts if these are a salient part of his social environment. Thus a person raised traditionally in a rural area may have traditional personality characteristics, but if forced to migrate to the city (and in the absence of group support for traditional behavior) may shift to the individualistic, calculating behavior characteristic of the purposive-rational mode—especially if there is sufficient contact with other adults having this latter outlook. Once the traditional mode has been replaced by the short-run hedonistic mode, i.e., lack of personal constraint, the transition to a purposive-rational mode becomes more difficult in later life. Children raised within a short-run hedonistic mode have made the transition to a purposive-rational mode only rarely, and then mainly through extremely close relationships with adults outside the home—teachers or ministers, for example. The unstable conditions of life in the lower class can engender the short-run hedonistic mode, implying the inability to plan.

For the second factor—the diffusion of knowledge of birth control—the mechanism may include fairly casual personal contacts, formalized contacts with physicians or other medical authorities, or even reading. Thus the rate of diffusion of knowledge of birth control should be substantially greater than that for the purposive-rational mode of orientation through the same society. This follows from the fact that the networks of casual contacts by an individual ordinarily are much broader and more inclusive than networks of close personal contacts. For the case of the small peasant village, however, the two networks are almost identical. Therefore diffusion of knowledge of birth control should be much slower in a society made up of such villages than in an urban society. Of course, literacy and comprehension of science accelerate this diffusion.

For the third value—the diffusion of values regarding ideal family size—description of a mechanism of diffusion is complicated by the decision process. Thus, for a given family, ideal family size may be a variable determined in part by diffusion through personal-contact mechanisms, but also by specific situational factors— income, health of wife, and so on. Insofar as a diffusion mechanism itself is involved, the relevant contacts tend to be more personal than needed to diffuse information, but less personal than those which diffuse personality characteristics. It is important to note that both decreases and increases of ideal family size may be diffused. "Fashion" may support either change.

For all three conditions a contact mechanism has been suggested, although "contacts" with various impersonal communication media are also important especially for the diffusion of information. To the extent that there are differential probabilities of contacts between various segments of society we may regard the social structure as placing constraints upon the channels of communication. If we had behavioral measures of the items on the Bogardus social-distance scale[7] for all the major segments of society then we would have an estimate of the amount of personal communication among these segments. The probabilities of intermarriage, social visiting, living in the same neighborhood, attending the same school, and working at the same job could all be determined.

Let us consider some research problems to which this scheme is applicable. In the United States there are three segments of the society whose fertility merits special attention: (1) rural fertility, (2) Negro fertility, and (3) fertility of certain religious groups, especially Catholic and Mormon. Each of these has tended to remain higher than the average in the general population. Each represents a different problem from the point of view of the theoretical scheme above.

The relatively high rural fertility of the past has been explained by all three of the reasons provided above: traditional orientation, lack of knowledge of birth control, and large ideal family size geared to farm production. All these factors should be greatly reduced in importance today. Farming as a production system has become rationalized, birth-control knowledge has diffused to rural areas, and mechanization of agricultural production has reduced the need for unskilled labor. It would be of some importance to design research to determine whether trends in rural fertility can be explained by the above factors, and precisely how these factors work together. I suspect that the diffusion of birth-control knowledge has come last and is the precipitating factor in fertility reduction.

The special case of Negro fertility will throw further light on the above problem, as we can contrast rural fertility with that of urban migrants from the rural areas. According to Bogue, Negro fertility in Chicago has remained much higher than expected, even for those Negro families that have been resident in Chicago for a number of years.[8] What we must do is determine the effects of segregation upon the diffusion processes. We wish to know whether the diffusion of birth-control knowledge is sufficient to bring about effective family planning, or if there must also be an acquisition of compulsive personality traits for family planning to become effective.

There are at least two relevant tests. First, we might compare Negroes who have close personal relationships with whites with those Negroes who have either casual contacts or no contacts with whites, holding social class and length of stay in the city constant. Second, we might compare Negro migrants with other recent rural migrant populations to see if degree of segregation within the city is a predictor of subsequent fertility behavior; the contrast with Southern rural whites might be the most appropriate. Rainwater argues that the short-run hedonistic mode of the urban lower class is the source of its high fertility behavior.[9] We would like to know if the Negro and white urban lower class are similar in this regard.

The third segment of the population we shall turn to is religiously defined. Both Catholics and Mormons have maintained relatively high fertility rates.[10] For Catholics, adherence to a traditional mode of orientation, especially when coupled with specific sanctions against modern methods of birth control, appears to be the proper explanation of the high fertility rates. But for Mormons, the religious support for large ideal family sizes appears to be the proper explanation. The test can come from comparing those families that plan with those families that do not plan. Among Catholics, planning families may use the rhythm method exclusively, or they may use modern methods that their church is opposed to. As to the Mormons, one would like to determine if users of modern birth control were more concerned with spacing of children than with limiting total family size. Research on rural orthodox Protestant denominations would be of great help in further assessment of the religious effect upon fertility. Two useful studies are of the Hutterites and of Appalachian fundamentalists.[11]

In summary, varying fertility rates are here viewed as a result of cultural constraints (the modes of orientation, social structural constraints), the channels of personal communication, the diffusion of relevant information and values in the context of these two constraints, and a two-person decision process.

We have previously established a basis for our social theories in the two major social-psychological studies of fertility. There have been a number of more recent studies. The members of the Indianapolis study research team divided into two groups which went somewhat separate ways in subsequent research, one group centered at Princeton, the other at Michigan.[12] From the point of view of the present theory both groups have retained the shortcomings of the Indianapolis study, although they have made modest advances in separate directions.

The Michigan group has focused on statements of ideal family size as a key predictor of fertility; they direct attention to such statements by adolescents as harbingers of trends. But they are not very explicit on questions that might suggest adjustment of these ideals according to major social changes. Thus they provide no way to adjust predictions for changes in income, in employment, social mobility, migration, and the like.

The Princeton group has focused on the prediction of the birth of a third child to a family that already has two children. Thus they are concentrating their attention on the adjustments of ideal family size and of fertility-control behavior at what they regard as the critical moment in family formation.

Both groups have broadened their samples to include Catholics and Jews as well as Protestants, but both are deficient for rural families and nonwhites. Thus it is not surprising that their main results bear on the significance of religion. The fact that economic conditions in the fifties differ from those measured in the Indianapolis study is largely ignored by both research groups.

The substance of both the Princeton and Michigan findings is that Catholic families are larger than Protestant families which in turn are larger than Jewish families. Mixed Catholic-Protestant families are halfway between Catholic and Protestant families, with the wife's religion exercising slightly greater weight than the husband's. Among Catholic families Italian background leads to much lower fertility than Irish background, irregular church attendance leads to much lower fertility, and the highest fertility is associated with wives that are graduates of Catholic colleges or universities.

The Princeton group itself is at a loss to interpret these findings. We have several tacks to take from our previous theory. First we note that our earlier discussion of occupation and urban-rural differences from diffusion would predict the main differences between religions. Thus we need to determine the extent to which religious differences may index time lags in diffusion of family planning and birth-control methods, the extent to which there is a specific religious effect in addition to the occupation and urban effect, and the extent to which there is a further religious effect on the goals of family planning—i.e., family-size ideals.

A specifically religious effect could represent either the degree of segregation of a religious group, as in a diffusion delay, or a separate source of diffusion of values. The differences between Protestants and Jews appear to be adequately explained by the effects of occupation and urban residence upon diffusion without additional appeal to specifically religious effects. The far higher occupational status of Jews and their far longer urban residence seem sufficient to account for their far more effective use of birth control and for their policies of restriction of family size to ensure adequate social status for their children. Discrimination against Jews in employment could lead to smaller families under the Banks hypothesis for two reasons: (1) The self-employed have a less certain income and hence must hedge in saving and planning; and (2) The need to protect children's employment implies greater educational expense. We shall return to this point when we discuss the differential influence of rural background upon Protestant fertility.

The differences between Catholics and Protestants are much more subtle. The research by Keyfitz on French Canadian fertility declines is our best evidence for diffusion from cities but within Catholic contacts.[13] The Princeton data bear on differences in birth-control use and in ideal family size. To consider the latter first, there is clear-cut evidence of higher ideal family-size preferences for Catholics than Protestants, yet one can ask if these preferences are not rationalizations for the inevitable consequences of Catholic-approved birth-control methods.

The Princeton data on birth control allow us to consider occupation and religion simultaneously. It is the contention of the research group that occupation differentials, so present in the Indianapolis study, are no longer relevant in the 1950's. My view is that their analysis does not support this conclusion. They do not separate their findings between planning and nonplanning groups as in the Indianapolis study. Recall that in the Indianapolis study only those couples that planned every pregnancy

Table 4-3 — First use of contraception, by religion and class*

FIRST USE OF CONTRACEPTION

Religion and class	Number	Before first birth	Between two births	After second birth	Still not using	Per cent total
Protestant						
White-collar	230	71	22	4	4	101
Blue-collar	243	51	34	9	6	100
Mixed Catholic						
White-collar	35	46	43	3	9	101
Blue-collar	51	45	37	4	14	100
Catholic						
White-collar	200	35	37	8	22	102
Blue-collar	281	39	36	7	17	99
Jewish						
White-collar	103	89	8	2	1	100
Blue-collar	22	86	5	5	5	101
Total	1,165	53	30	6	11	100

* Charles F. Westoff, Robert G. Potter, Jr., Philip C. Sagi, and Elliot G. Mishler, *Family Growth in Metropolitan America* (Princeton, N. J.: Princeton U. P., 1961), Table 7, p. 72.

were retained as planners in the final resume and that the interesting theoretical results occurred only within this special group. If we look at their table, First Use of Contraception by Religion and Class (Table 4-3), we find results that support both the Indianapolis study and my own interpretation of that study from the perspective of the Weber-Banks hypothesis. Only 53 per cent of the sample used contraception before the first birth. Occupation differences among Protestants (white-collar 71 per cent, blue-collar 51 per cent) are much as one would expect in this urban sample given continued diffusion of planning over the sixteen-year time gap of the interviews. Further, we know from the Puerto Rican study that use of contraception does not suffice to describe a couple as a planning family; regularity of use and number of years of use are also necessary. But since the Princeton sample did not include families with births in excess of their ideal family size, we learn little about the relationship between family planning and birth control.

The absence of occupation differences among Jews (white-collar 89 per cent, blue-collar 86 per cent) can be explained simply by the fact that diffusion of family planning is complete within this group; we expect such completion due to the long history of urban residence.

The absence of occupation differences among Catholics on first use of contraception is a more interesting phenomenon. We note first that there is a slight inverse relationship (white-collar 35 per cent, blue-collar 39 per cent). Next we may recall the segregation hypothesis for rates of diffusion. The Michigan group found that Catholics educated in Catholic schools had quite different fertility preferences from Catholics with secular education; within the Princeton data, however, the influence of Catholic colleges on Catholic women were found to be much more important than any other aspect of Catholic education. Thus if we assume that the Catholic wives with Catholic college education are more likely to have white-collar husbands than blue-collar husbands, we can account for the slight inverse relationship. These data thus support the segregation hypothesis and the hypothesis of a separate source of values maintained within Catholic women's colleges. This line of thought is reinforced by Table 11 on page 79 of Westoff et al., *Family Growth in Metropolitan Areas*, describing the distribution of methods of contraception. The rhythm method is popular only with Catholics, and is much more popular with white-collar Catholics than blue-collar Catholics (white-collar 49 per cent, blue-collar 29 per cent). The rhythm method was the only birth-control method approved by Pope Pius XII in his 1939 statement.

We still do not have definite evidence on the effect of Catholic methods of birth control upon Catholic ideal family size, though the apparent independent influence of Catholic education is such that the two effects would have to operate together. There is some evidence that bears on this point, however. We must note that such rationalization might occur in statements of ideal family size at the time of marriage, or it might occur after the experience of two or three births. In a recent Michigan study the fluctuation of family-size expectations between successive interviews is much greater among Catholics.[14] It is interesting to note that Catholics educated in secular schools change more than Catholics educated in Catholic schools, thus implying the importance of segregation in Catholic behavior.

Now we must note that the sequential adjustment of ideal family size could be predicted from a Banks hypothesis on changes in expected future income. Both the Princeton group and the Michigan group have partial evidence on this point. These groups do not actually estimate future income. They obtain present income and present occupation, show that occupation is a better predictor of ideal family size for planners, and then discount income. But I would regard present occupation of employed males under age 35 as a better predictor of expected future income than present income. The Princeton group found as an effect of the 1958 recession that a reduction in income reduced fertility, but unemployment actually appeared to increase it. Since unemployment occurred at the lowest occupation levels with least planning capabilities, the second finding was discounted by them. The Michigan group, using the Detroit Area Study from 1960–63, came to the same conclusion on the effect of unemployment, but completely discounted change of income. I interpret their Table 6[15] differently however, for the most frequent reason given for reducing expectations in this table is financial (17 per cent of downward change). They comment that this is a small per cent, but give no evidence that it should be any larger—i.e., no evidence that a larger group should have expected or experienced a decline in income. The aggregated income changes in the United States as a whole and in Detroit for that time period were not downward, so the number of persons experiencing decline of income should not be large.

Further support for the Banks hypothesis is contained in a special study by Westoff, Kelly, and Mishler of a follow-up of a group of college graduates who had been initially interviewed while students, then subsequently interviewed twenty years later.[16] Within this group the lower the occupational status the greater the gap between marriage and the first child, and the gap between first child and second child. I interpret this finding as a result of differences in expected future income; the lower occupations in this sample are likely to have fairly flat income curves and a fairly high amount of employment security (civil service jobs), while the higher occupations are likely to have very substantial increases in income at the ages when the cost of college education for children is incurred. Thus if we assume that everyone in this sample desires a college education for his children, then cautious spacing in the light of budget considerations should be more evident for those who must save to meet the expense and cannot afford too many children in college at one time.

Evidence on the influence of rural background was

assembled by Goldberg,[17] and more recently by Duncan.[18] With the Indianapolis study sample (Protestants only), Goldberg is able to show that the relation between fertility and occupation largely reflects a relation between fertility and rural origin. I simply interpret his finding as evidence for the diffusion of family planning across occupation and out from cities. Using a national sample that does not allow religious differentiation, Duncan shows an influence of rural background, but he also demonstrates that social class (as measured by education) has an independent effect, thus substantiating the notion of diffusion here presented. He has an interesting anomaly in his relation of education with fertility that can be resolved by the theory that we have developed here. As education of wife increases, fertility decreases within all residence categories, but as education of husband increases there is a reversal at the college level with an implication of increased fertility. I interpret the wife's education as an index of diffusion of family planning that is especially necessary, given the kinds of cooperation and comprehension required to employ the typical Western methods of birth control successfully (Banks emphasized this point in his discussion of the spread of contraceptive information in Victorian England). I interpret the husband's education as an index of expected future income. Thus planning couples (assuming college-educated husbands are largely married to college-educated wives and are thereby part of planning couples) adjust fertility according to their expected future incomes.

Further evidence for the influence of rural backgrounds upon the diffusion of family planning is furnished by De Jong in a study of fertility in Western Kentucky.[19] Here the relative absence of family planning was found to be strongly associated with Protestant fundamentalist beliefs that such activities were sinful, both in the mountain areas and in large cities which have been receiving migrants from these areas.

Note that Keyfitz's findings on trends in rural French-Canadian fertility are suggestive of the link between rural ways of life. Differential fertility implied that diffusion took place among the segregated French, apparently from the city outward.

Additional evidence supporting this argument comes from a series of studies in the Near-East and Asia. The diffusion of knowledge and interest in birth-control techniques follows the pattern we would expect from Banks—the highly urbanized professionals come first. Further, the religious boundaries are revealed, with "modernization" having the expected effect. Finally, the significance of communication between husband and wife is brought out, both in the relation between wife's education and fertility and in direct communication questions.

The six studies of interest represent a wide variety of social and cultural conditions. In particular they represent very different stages of modernization. Studies by Driver[20] and by Sinha[21] in India found little evidence of new fertility patterns even in urban areas. The Mysore study in India,[22] and studies by Abu-Lughod[23] and by Rizk[24] in Egypt, detect the beginnings of new fertility trends in the urbanized professional classes. The study by Yaukey[25] in Lebanon reveals modernization trends well under way.

Even when there is little modernization apparent in fertility patterns, there is an incipient change revealed by attitude and information measures. Knowledge of birth control and family planning, as well as favorable attitudes toward them, are associated with professional occupations, higher incomes, higher education, and membership in minority religions in both the Driver and Sinha studies. Note that, in both of these studies, the only strong social correlate of low fertility is the education of the wife. Considering all those couples aware and favorably disposed, the implementation of family planning evidently occurs first within couples with highly educated wives. I interpret this finding as evidence for the importance of the communication process between husband and wife, especially communication on sex from a scientific standpoint. As a final note, the highest fertility found by Sinha for any education category, husband or wife, is the privately educated, suggesting that these people are least susceptible to the diffusion of modernization.

Table 4-4 — Central India: Attitudes toward family planning and their implementation*

A. Percentage of Couples Having Knowledge of Birth-Control Techniques and Interested in Family Limitation, by Residence

| | | Percentage of couples | | | | | |
| | | KNOWLEDGE | | | INTEREST | | |
Residence	Number of couples	Some	None	Total	Some	None	Total
City	882	46.6	53.4	100.0	78.4	21.6	100.0
Town	309	27.8	72.2	100.0	72.2	27.8	100.0
Village	1123	25.1	74.9	100.0	64.0	36.0	100.0
Total	2314	33.7	66.3	100.0	70.3	29.7	100.0

B. Mean Number of Children Ever Born to Couples Classified by Residence and Age of Wife

Age of Wife (in years)	City (882)	Town (309)	Village (1123)	Total (2314)
Under 25	1.9	1.7	1.7	1.8
25–34	3.8	4.2	4.2	4.0
35–44	5.7	6.2	6.3	6.0
45 or more	6.6	7.1	6.3	6.5
All Ages				
Arithmetic	4.4	4.5	4.6	4.5
Weighted	4.4	4.7	4.6	4.5

Table 4-4 (Continued) — Central India: Attitudes toward family planning and their implementation*

C. Percentage of Couples Having Knowledge of Birth-Control Techniques and Interested in Family Limitation, by Education of Wife

		Percentage of couples					
	Number of	KNOWLEDGE			INTEREST		
Educational level	couples	Some	None	Total	Some	None	Total
None	1772	23.7	76.3	100.0	63.9	36.1	100.0
Primary	318	59.1	40.9	100.0	83.0	17.0	100.0
Above Primary	224	76.3	23.7	100.0	95.5	4.5	100.0
Total	2314	33.7	66.3	100.0	70.3	29.7	100.0

D. Mean Number of Children Ever Born to Couples Classified by Education and Age of Wife

Age of wife (in years)	No Education (1772)	Primary School (318)	Above primary School (224)	Total (2314)
Under 25	1.8	1.7	1.6	1.8
25–34	4.2	4.0	3.2	4.0
35–44	6.1	6.4	4.8	6.0
45 or more	6.5	6.8	6.2	6.5
All Ages				
Arithmetic	4.7	4.3	3.4	4.5
Weighted	4.6	4.7	3.8	4.5

* Tables selected from Edwin C. Driver, *Differential Fertility in Central India* (Princeton, N. J.: Princeton U. P., 1963), Tables 74, 90, 112, and 120.

The two studies in Egypt further reinforce our argument. Abu-Lughod shows from 1960 Cairo census data that education of wife is the most significant social variable related to declining fertility, and that this is a continuation of a trend first discerned by El-Badry[26] in the 1947 census data. The census data are supplemented by social psychological surveys as summarized by Rizk. She documents the importance of birth control in this decline, and shows that the use of birth control is most common among the younger urban highly educated couples, declining very sharply as one goes down the social-class system within the city or out to semiurban or village areas.

Figure 4–2

Cairo, Egypt: Fertility Differentials by Education of Wife, 1960
(Median number of live births to currently married women, by education of wife and duration of marriage)

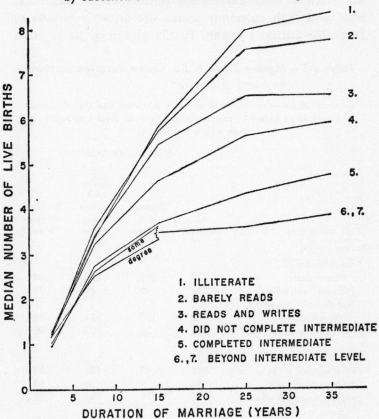

I. ILLITERATE
2. BARELY READS
3. READS AND WRITES
4. DID NOT COMPLETE INTERMEDIATE
5. COMPLETED INTERMEDIATE
6.,7. BEYOND INTERMEDIATE LEVEL

Source: Janet Abu-Lughod, "The Emergence of Differential Fertility in Urban Egypt," *Milbank Memorial Fund Quarterly*, Vol. XLIII, No. 2, Part I (April 1965), Figure 1, p. 238.

The Mysore study in India brings out these contrasts even more clearly. In Bangalore City a Western fertility pattern is clearly seen, but the surrounding towns and villages do not yet show any indication of this pattern. Thus there is an inverse relationship between social status and fertility in Bangalore City, in contrast to a direct relationship in the surrounding area. Again education is the strongest social correlate of fertility. High educational level and high economic status are strongly related to favorable attitudes toward family planning. In addition

Table 4-5 — Mysore State, India: Communication between husband and wife*

(Association between responses of married women and their husbands to questions on extent of communication between them with regard to their desire for children)

		RESPONSE OF WOMAN		
Zone and response of husband	All responses	Discussed with husband	Not discussed but husband's views known	Husband's views not known
Bangalore City				
Total number of respondents	734	272	278	184
Discussed with wife	222	92	74	56
Not discussed but wife's views known	272	105	101	66
Wife's views not known	240	75	103	62
Zone III (Rural plains)				
Total number of respondents	302	43	131	128
Discussed with wife	54	9	30	15
Not discussed but wife's views known	118	19	47	52
Wife's views not known	130	15	54	61

* United Nations, Department of Economic and Social Affairs, *The Mysore Population Study* (New York: United Nations, 1961), Table 11.28, p. 156.

we have detailed information on the amount and quality of communication about family planning between husband and wife, especially as it relates to knowledge of birth control. "In Bangalore City, only 13 per cent of the couples agreed, in the responses of both husband and wife, that the question had been discussed between them, and in the rural area the corresponding figure was only 3 per cent,"[27] the "question" having to do with regard to their desires for children. A larger proportion of persons with high school or college education reported discussions or knowledge of the spouse's view. Knowledge of any birth-control methods was low, but associated with high education and young age. Western methods were little known and little used except among the most highly educated.

Only in the Lebanon study do we see fertility patterns that can truly be described as Western. Yaukey provides us with a fine summary table in which the influences of education, religion, and residence on fertility are simultaneously revealed. The Christians are quite Western-oriented through long contacts with France and more recently with the United States. Thus we find the lowest fertility among urban educated Christians, next lowest with urban uneducated Christians, next urban educated Moslems, and so on. It seems that modernization first appeared in the urban educated Christian group and spread from them to the uneducated Christians (analogous to Keyfitz' evidence for diffusion among French Canadians), the appearance of modernization among urban educated Moslems was later, and diffusion to the urban uneducated Moslems has only begun. This view is further supported by the data for the median first pregnancy delayed by conception control. An interesting detail, however, is that once Moslems begin using con-

Table 4-6 — Lebanon: Summary of main differences in birth-control behavior among social background types‡

| | VILLAGE | | CITY | | | |
Social background type*	Uneducated Moslem	Christian	Uneducated Moslem	Christian	Educated Moslem	Christian
Total fertility rate	7.43	8.16	7.35	4.14	5.56	3.44
Per cent ever inducing abortion†	2	0	13	20	31	26
Per cent ever using any method of conception control†	2	16	60	56	83	86
Median first pregnancy delayed by conception control†	—	7.7	4.9	3.6	3.2	2.4
Per cent ever using appliance methods of conception control†	0	0	34	27	60	49

* Refers to highest level of education achieved by either member of couple.

† Based on women married ten years or more.

‡ David Yaukey, *Fertility Differences in a Modernizing Country* (Princeton, N. J.: Princeton U. P., 1961), Table VI–5, p. 70.

ception control, they are less inhibited from abortion or from appliance methods, suggesting an effect of orthodox Christian teaching. This point is brought out by comparing urban educated Moslems with urban educated Christians.

Let us now review the overall implications of this chapter. It has been our intention to show that the research on birth rates and fertility reviewed in Chapter 2 and the social-psychological research reviewed in this chapter can be interpreted from a single theoretical perspective. We hope that the plausibility of our theoretical perspective has been established by this review and critique of the research literature; we further hope that the marked differences of this interpretation from other interpretations have been made sufficiently clear so that they may inspire appropriate further research in fertility. If the Weber-Banks hypothesis has substantial merit, it can be used to develop population projections conditional upon social parameters. The techniques for such population projections are indicated in the Appendix.

Our attention has been focused on social-psychological aspects of the demographic transition—the diffusion of planning. We should also summarize the implication of our argument for the post-transition society, for example, contemporary United States.

Two recent trends in U.S. birth rates have attracted attention. The baby boom of the late 1940's and 1950's was entirely unexpected by demographers. In the 1960's, however, a gradual decline of births has emerged. These phenomena may be described in terms of annual birth rates, average family size, and birth probabilities to women with specified numbers of previous children.

The baby boom was first revealed in high postwar annual birth rates. As such it seemed to represent a postponement of birth from the depression and war years, as well as the initiation of a large number of new families from the large number of newly formed or reconstituted families. In other words, the annual births were mostly made up of first and second births. Under the assumption that the ultimate family sizes of the 1930's were still preferred, demographers expected few births of third and higher order, and therefore predicted a sharp decline in annual births in the early 1950's. Instead, annual births remained high throughout the 1950's.

Studies of the birth probabilities and the average family sizes in the 1950's revealed three things. First, there was a completely different pattern associated with the new generation of families. Postponement of births from the Depression was not an important factor in the new annual births; instead, families initially formed in the 1930's continued to fulfill their original small-family ideals, while families formed after the war revealed closer spacing and larger ultimate goals.

Second, the larger ultimate goals were associated with a shift to a preference for three to five children in a family; both the very small and very large families were out of fashion. Third, these new goals were almost universal, the classic differentials by region, residence, class, and other social-status characteristics had all narrowed, leaving religion and race as the only important social distinctions.

It is worth noting that the postwar rise in annual births was common to most Western nations, followed by declines as demographers had expected; the declines were slowest in coming to the United States, Canada, and Holland. All three nations have historically been Protestant yet have large and growing Catholic populations. Further research on the religious effect might help us understand the similarities among these nations.

Let us return to our theory for interpretation of these phenomena. Banks' hypothesis suggests that general economic conditions in the postwar period had a strong effect on family patterns. This effect would permit the increase of family size, but not without limits. The continued spread of family planning would have the effect of eliminating the very large unplanned family, and thus decreasing annual births. These two effects taken together can partly account for the rise in births followed by the slight declines of the 1960's.

But three phenomena require additional attention. First, we must know more about the upper limits on ideal family size during general prosperity; second, we must account for the unpopularity of the very small family;

and third, we must consider sensitivity of birth rates to changes in overall economic structure and changes in the customs surrounding family formation. Automation and selective unemployment in particular must be discussed.

Following Banks, the upper limits might come from the costs of social mobility for children, especially the educational costs. Direct social-psychological inquiry would be needed to establish the importance of this factor and precisely how it operates in the different social strata. Other possibilities for an upper limit include a localized Malthusian effect from overcrowding within the housing unit (much postwar housing has been of the small-family suburban type, especially in the large developments) and a change in the employment patterns of married women that involves resuming a career after age 30 which was interrupted for childbearing.

The unpopularity of the very small family may be traceable to personal revulsion on the part of the parents who were themselves only children, although efforts to document this view with data have always been disappointing. More likely lines of thought stem from two cultural phenomena of the postwar era. One is the emergence of bureaucratic structures as the typical social environment for all activities. Such popular writers as David Riesman[28] and William H. Whyte[29] see various trends toward group conformity; perhaps the easiest way to join a group is to have a family. Perhaps the influence of the war, with its disruption of social ties, is a more likely source of social and cultural pressures toward familism. If the war was more important than bureaucracy, then we could predict a fading effect of such social pressures toward familism as new generations of families are being formed in the late 1950's and 1960's.

Automation and related changes in occupation and

employment suggest that the family formation and birth rates of the marginal employee may be influenced. In particular this view suggests selective impact upon persons recently entering the labor market with insufficient skills, and upon the nonwhites (last-hired, first-fired). The former condition might imply that high school dropouts and persons with high school education only might delay family formation and postpone births. From our previous theory we might suspect that high school dropouts are incapable of such decision making (are acting in the short-run hedonistic mode of orientation); we would therefore focus our attention on the high school graduate. However, for high school dropouts and for nonwhites we might make special studies of the prevalence of illegitimate births and of family dissolution—especially separation.

NOTES

1. Pascal K. Whelpton and Clyde V. Kiser (eds.), *Social and Psychological Factors Affecting Fertility*, Vols. I–V (New York: Milbank Memorial Fund, 1946–58). These volumes contain reprints of a series of articles originally published in the *Milbank Memorial Fund Quarterly*.

2. Reuben Hill, J. Mayone Stycos, and Kurt Back, *The Family and Population Control* (Chapel Hill, N.C.: U. of North Carolina Press, 1959).

3. Whelpton and Kiser, *op. cit.*, Vol. 5, pp. 1325–69. This article was originally published in *Milbank Memorial Fund Quarterly*, XXXVI, No. 3 (July 1958), 282–329.

4. *Ibid.*, pp. 1355–6.

5. Paul K. Hatt, *Backgrounds of Human Fertility in Puerto Rico* (Princeton, N.J.: Princeton U. P., 1952).

6. Albert K. Cohen, *Delinquent Boys* (New York: Free Press, 1963).

7. Emery S. Bogardus, "A Social Distance Scale," *Sociology and Social Research*, XVII (1933), pp. 265–71.

8. D. J. Bogue and D. P. Dandekar, *Population Trends and Prospects for The Chicago-Northwestern Indiana Consolidated*

Metropolitan Area: 1960–1990 (Chicago: Population Research and Training Center, University of Chicago, 1962), pp. 11–14.

9. Lee Rainwater, *And The Poor Get Children* (Chicago: Quadrangle Books, 1960).

10. Wilson H. Grabill, Clyde V. Kiser, and Pascal K. Whelpton, *The Fertility of American Women* (New York: Wiley, 1958), p. 280; Ralph Thomlinson, *Population Dynamics* (New York: Random House, 1965), p. 179.

11. Gordon F. De Jong, "Religious Fundamentalism, Socio-Economic Status, and Fertility Attitudes in the Southern Appalachians," *Demography*, II (1965), 540–8; Joseph W. Eaton and Albert J. Mayer, "The Social Biology of Very High Fertility Among the Hutterites," *Human Biology*, XXV, No. 3 (September 1953), 206–64, reprinted in *Man's Capacity to Reproduce: The Demography of a Unique Population* (New York: Free Press, 1954).

12. Princeton group publications include Charles F. Westoff, Robert G. Potter, and Philip C. Sagi, "Some Selected Findings of the Princeton Fertility Study: 1963," *Demography*, I, No. 1 (1964), 130–5; *ibid., The Third Child* (Princeton, N.J.: Princeton U. P., 1963); Charles F. Westoff and Elliott G. Mishler, *Family Growth in Metropolitan America* (Princeton, N.J.: Princeton U. P., 1961). Michigan group publications include Ronald Freedman, Lolagene C. Coombs, and Larry Bumpass, "Stability and Change in Expectations about Family Size: A Longitudinal Study," *Demography*, II (1965), 250–75; Ronald Freedman, David Goldberg, and Doris Slesinger, "Current Fertility Expectations of Married Couples in the United States," *Population Index*, XXIX, No. 4 (October 1963), 366–91; Ronald Freedman, P. K. Whelpton, and A. A. Campbell, *Family Planning, Sterility and Population Growth* (New York: McGraw-Hill, 1959).

13. Nathan Keyfitz, "A Factorial Arrangement of Comparisons of Family Size," *American Journal of Sociology*, LVIII (March 1953), 470–9, reprinted in P. K. Hatt and A. J. Reiss, Jr. (eds.), *Cities and Society* (New York: Free Press, 1957).

14. Freedman, Coombs, Bumpass, *op. cit.*

15. *Ibid.*, p. 261.

16. Charles F. Westoff, Elliott G. Mishler, and E. Lowell Kelly, "Preferences in Size of Family and Eventual Fertility Twenty Years After," *American Journal of Sociology*, LXII (March 1957), 491–7.

17. David Goldberg, "The Fertility of Two-Generation Urbanites," *Population Studies*, XII (March 1959), 214–22, and David Goldberg, "Another Look at the Indianapolis Fertility Data,"

Milbank Memorial Fund Quarterly, XXXVIII (January 1960), 23–6.

18. Otis Dudley Duncan, "Farm Background and Differential Fertility," *Demography*, II (1965), 240–9.

19. Gordon F. De Jong, "Religious Fundamentalism, Socio-Economic Status, and Fertility Attitudes in the Southern Appalachians," *Demography*, II (1965), 540–8.

20. Edwin C. Driver, *Differential Fertility in Central India* (Princeton, N.J.: Princeton U. P., 1963).

21. Note on fertility by J. N. Sinha in Radhakamal Mukerjee and Baljit Singh, *Social Profiles of a Metropolis* (New York: Asia Publishing House, 1961).

22. United Nations, *The Mysore Study* (New York: United Nations, 1963).

23. Janet Abu-Lughod, "The Emergence of Differential Fertility in Urban Egypt," *Milbank Memorial Fund Quarterly*, XLIII, No. 2, Part 1 (April 1965), 235–53.

24. Hanna Rizk, "Social and Psychological Factors Affecting Fertility in the United Arab Republic," *Marriage and Family Living*, XXV, No. 1 (February 1963).

25. David Yaukey, *Fertility Differences in a Modernizing Country* (Princeton, N.J.: Princeton U. P., 1961).

26. M. A. El-Badry, "Some Aspects of Fertility in Egypt," *Milbank Memorial Fund Quarterly*, XXXIV, No. 1 (January 1956).

27. United Nations, *op. cit.*, p. 156.

28. David Riesman, *The Lonely Crowd* (New Haven: Yale U. P., 1950).

29. William H. Whyte, Jr., *The Organization Man* (New York: Simon and Schuster, 1957).

CHAPTER 5

Migration

W E wish now to review the migration-research literature in a manner analogous to the review of fertility in the previous chapter. Our purpose is to demonstrate the consistency of a theory of migration with research findings. In so doing we hope to bring out the contrast between migration and fertility as behavioral consequences of decision processes, thus clarifying the implications of the more general theoretical notions that we have been using. We shall consider the research derivative from census data as well as the research using social-psychological methods.

We shall concentrate on migration within national boundaries, sometimes called internal migration. Thus we shall give a secondary place to the major international migrations that have been inspired by political and religious conflict. These migrations are very important, but we cannot develop a theory that predicts political and religious conflict here.

Suppose we have a set of persons, each of whom can be characterized by his place of usual residence. Suppose further that these places of usual residence can be assigned to geographical areas. As time passes the persons can change their place of usual residence; such a change will be defined as a move. For any given set of geographical areas we may define the internal migration as those moves that cross the boundaries of areas in the set but originate and terminate in areas in the set. The total internal migration is composed of migration streams. Each migration stream has one area in the set as an origin, and one area as a destination. Let us define the case where a person retains his residence in the same area, whether or not he moves within that area, as a stream (the reflexive stream). Then for n areas we have n^2 streams. These streams may be used to represent the cells of a matrix whose rows list all areas designated as origins and whose columns list all areas designated as destinations.

We would like to predict, for any given time period, the numbers of persons in the migration streams over a set of areas. These numbers of persons can be seen as entries in the cells of the matrix of streams. For example, if we take a year as a time period, then the entries in the matrix of streams correspond to the number of persons whose places of usual residence at the beginning of the year were in the areas defined by the rows, and whose place of usual residence at the end of the year was in areas defined by the columns. We shall consider the number of persons in each stream to be the volume of the stream.

We know from previous research that such predictions should utilize information on the social characteristics of the persons and the social characteristics of the areas. We would like to use this information in such a way that we predict not only the volumes of the streams but the social characteristics of the streams as well.

We also know from previous research that such predictions should take into account the particular set of geographic areas over which the streams are defined. The size of the areas and the delineation of the boundaries of the areas influence both the volume and characteristics of the migration streams defined over the areas. We would like to take account of these characteristics of areas appropriately in our predictions.[1]

Thus, for any given set of areas, we would like to predict the volume and characteristics of the migration streams. Further, we wish to specify the form of the prediction conditional upon the delineation of the areas.

We shall predict the occurrence of migration in a given time period as the outcome of a process of decision making under social constraints. In particular we will consider the case of a family that is headed by a married man who has already entered the labor force. We shall assume that migration is a result of a decision process within the family, and that the decision process is constrained on one hand by the characteristics of the family and its constituent individuals, and on the other by labor markets, commuting patterns, and housing markets.

We wish to predict the area of residence next year for a person with a particular area of residence this year and a particular set of social characteristics. If we also take account of the changes in his social characteristics, then we can repeat the prediction in succeeding years. If these predictions are summed over all persons in a given set of areas then they define the volume and characteristics of all streams of migration among all areas (including the nonmigrants). If the streams themselves are summed over all areas of destination, including nonmigrants as a reflexive stream, then we obtain the predicted size and characteristics of the population of each area.

We shall represent the prediction as the outcome of decision processes that are constrained by modes of orientation, social variables, and social-psychological decision processes. In contrast with fertility, however, we find that the locus of decision-making authority is more complex. With fertility we could assume that the decision-making process was primarily centered in the married couple, but with migration we have cases in which larger organizations can dictate moves to persons that cannot readily be rejected by the persons—for example, the case of military organizations. To do complete justice to this phenomenon we should expand our theory to include the decision-making processes in large organizations, but it is impossible to treat such theories within the confines of this book, and it is very difficult to ascertain the empirical consequences of these kinds of moves as there is practically no research literature bearing on the point. Therefore we shall concentrate our attention upon the decision of individuals, particularly the joint-decision process in the family. We shall try to introduce organizational effects as constraints upon these family-decision processes.

Let us first consider the influence of the Weberian modes of orientation upon migration. We shall again assume that a purposive-rational mode of orientation has diffused outward from the professional classes. Associated with this mode of orientation is the capacity to make extensive calculations of consequences of alternatives, including consequences far in the future, and the capacity to adhere to a plan of action that will attain these future goals, sometimes called deferred gratification. In contrast, the traditional mode involves strong customary constraints on decisions, while the short-run hedonistic mode exists in the absence of the influence of customs but lacks the elaborate future orientation of the purposive-rational mode. We shall interpret kinship influences and the phenomenon of squatting from these modes.

Let us trace through the decision processes associated with the purposive-rational mode of orientation, then return to the other modes subsequently. As with fertility we find that, for a family, the main constraints stem from characteristics of the husband's job and from characteristics of the household. In contrast to fertility, however, the husband's expected income is less important than other characteristics of his job, and the important characteristics of the household are the life-cycle, or family-growth, characteristics such as number of children and their age. Thus we would expect fertility patterns to influence migration.

The implications of job and household characteristics turn on the special characteristics of the social psychological joint decision-making process. We shall argue that the husband and wife partition the decision process such that the husband specifies the job related constraints on moving while the wife specifies the household related constraints on moving. These are the constraints on whether to move, and if so, where? We shall further argue that the husband's constraints define an area bounded by commuting distance and partitioned by housing cost, whereas the wife's constraints are specific to neighborhoods and the detailed characteristics of the houses. Thus the wife's constraints operate within bounds set by the husband's constraints; the wife's influence is greatest at the small scale.

Let us consider the husband's constraints first. There are two that must be considered in migration that we could neglect in fertility. First there is the degree to which specific jobs and specific areas are linked. Two cases occur here—one in which the performance of skills is localized and the other in which capital investment associated with the job is localized (not transferable to other areas as in a "practice" for a doctor). The localization of performance of skills was once dominated by the costs of transportation of raw materials associated with work, or with the costs of communication throughout an organization. Thus the phenomena of industrial cities, political cities, and religious cities emerged along with the commercial cities. But the costs of transportation and communication have been driven steadily downward to the point that only very specialized kinds of communication are regarded as having localized significance—for example, education, as related to industrial parks located near universities.

The geographical extension of the labor market, i.e., the dispersion of knowledge of jobs, is the main constraint on movement of individuals. In general, the higher the skills of the occupation (within blue-collar and within white-collar occupations) the more geographically extended the job market. Thus higher skills are associated with longer moves.

The localization of capital investment associated with job depends in part upon the organization context in which the job is performed. If the capital investment is held by a corporation, with the job itself salaried, then this case—the salaried person—has already been considered above. But if the income depends upon the performance of the corporation itself, then the transferability of assets becomes crucial—if you can't sell your property, you are stuck with it. Selling alone is not sufficient; one also must be able to acquire similar property at a different location. The difficult cases occur when personal contacts are an important aspect of the business; these are the least transferable assets. Thus the small entrepreneur and the free professional are mired down in localities (and therefore have lost the freedom that they hoped to attain by "being their own boss").

Second, there is the career, the existence of a sequence of jobs such that the attainment of a future job objective requires a certain pattern of preliminary educational and job experiences. It is in the light of the career that a person acting in a purposive-rational mode can accept lower salaries or less satisfactory working conditions over a short run in order to achieve other kinds of job satisfactions over a long run. Different occupations have different career implications.

A third job-related characteristic is income. We must consider expected future income in relation to the cost of housing. Income constraints should place an upper bound on housing in the sense that a number of alternatives are eliminated because they are too expensive. The income constraints are articulated through transfer of assets in a manner similar to the transfer of business property. In this case the difference between renting and owning is crucial. In renting, transfer of assets has a minimal cost, and in particular a minimal risk, but in selling, the costs of transfer of assets depend upon the local housing markets at both ends of the move, with ordinarily a high degree of risk. However, we have to relate budget making to desired standard of living, and here we must consider the standard of living desired for children in the future as well as that desired for the parents themselves. For these aspects I have already argued that the wife plays a critical role in decision making. Thus we should now shift to the household characteristics in order to further specify our theory.

The first household characteristic we should consider is the number and spacing of children. The relevant predictions of births have been considered in the previous chapter. For the migration aspect we need to know how housing decisions are influenced. There are two kinds of influence—the degree to which the costs of transporting large numbers of children serve as an impediment to moving, and the constraints upon new housing. Both kinds, however, respond to the changes in family composition. The addition of babies, the need for schools and recreation, and then the departure of the children—these are the factors that define the life cycle of the family and constrain the housing needs.

The implications of the life cycle for housing choice can be specified only in the context of the desired standard of living mentioned above. The housing unit is part of a status-seeking strategy. It is usually the largest single investment of the family. Thus the definition of desirable housing includes calculation of an appropriate symbol display for the family as well as calculation of status-seeking activities that will be facilitated by the acquisition of a particular housing unit. The latter point may be illustrated by the effort to obtain "appropriate" playmates for one's children by obtaining housing in particular neighborhoods, e.g., pure-white neighborhoods. If the parents' status aspirations for their daughters are expressed by trying to influence the selection of marriage partners, we would expect the greatest expenditure on symbol display to occur during the adolescence of the daughters. Indeed, we might expect a family with sons to maximize on their educational attainments while a family with daughters would maximize on housing and related social activities.

Aside from the factors mentioned above we should expect a diffuse influence of preferences for particular climates and particular kinds of activities upon residential location. Thus opportunities for outdoor as well as evening recreation will exert some influence upon decision making after the constraints discussed above have been satisfied. For example, the greatest influence of these factors in U.S. data is seen for retired persons, for whom the job and household constraints have ceased to be relevant. Note that some kinds of recreation are found far from cities, whereas other kinds of recreation are found only in cities.

Now let us return to the traditional mode of orientation. Here we are seeking to understand the influence of customs upon migration. Now, aside from nomads and practitioners of slash-and-burn agriculture, the bulk of the traditional population is in settled agricultural villages with a strong customary bias against leaving the community. If, however, these people are forced to move, the same customs encourage their moving *en bloc*, thus preserving the social unit that reinforces the traditional customs.[2] Such agricultural villages have a social structure strongly organized around kinship patterns, so we would expect the influence of kinship to emerge in patterns of migration, either internal or across political boundaries. In the United States we have seen such migration of peasant populations from Europe to America, from Puerto Rico and Mexico to

America, and from the rural south to the urban north.[3] In each case the immigrants have attempted to reestablish the pattern of village settlement, some by going directly to agricultural settlements (Pennsylvania Dutch), and others by seeking to create ethnic villages in the cities.[4] To the extent that the new migrants are met by segregation, their communal ties are reenforced and are more likely to be transmitted across generational lines. Religion can serve as a symbolic rallying point for this type of urban community. Patriarchal authority also is characteristic of such communities.

In the event that a traditional population is forced to move, perhaps from overpopulation of the agricultural sector of an economy, two intermediate kinds of activities can occur short of complete relocation. One is the phenomenon of the young males seeking employment in other areas yet returning at regular intervals in hopes of resettling in their native villages. The other is the related phenomenon of "squatting"—acquiring highly temporary housing for the family—especially evident in mild climates.[5] Either of these alternatives raises the possibility of breakdown of the traditional customs.

The breakdown of the traditional customs ordinarily leads to action in the short-run hedonistic mode of orientation; in other words, squatting becomes endemic, and temporary adjustment becomes a way of life. So long as erratic employment reinforces this world view, then prediction of migration must follow from a knowledge of immediate situational factors, such as localized overcrowding. A degeneration of family formation can often follow, with forms of consensual marriage and temporary union of adults becoming dominant. Thus the possibilities of family decision making are greatly reduced, and, insofar as clusters of children have female family heads, the characteristics of female employment can come to dominate family decision making. With small and irregular incomes the possibilities for systematic status seeking are greatly reduced, and ordinarily survival on a day-to-day basis becomes the dominant social motive.

Let us now relate the theoretical discussion to research. Procedures for the testing of this theory depend upon the size of areas with reference to which change of residence is defined, as well as certain boundary characteristics of these areas. If the areas are drawn so as to contain clusters of commuting trips, as one hopes for the Standard Metropolitan Statistical Areas used by the U.S. Bureau of the Census, then moves between these areas must imply job change, and therefore the job-change aspects of the theory must be sustained by the data. If the areas fall within many overlapping commuting rings, a move must imply housing change, and therefore the housing aspects of the theory must be sustained by the data; blocks are an example of such areas. Although housing change is also implied by the moves across large areas, there is no way of testing the housing-change aspects of the theory, as it only explains location within commuting rings; such locations are not identified by these area boundaries. The implications of job markets and of housing markets are both masked, to some degree, by the size and boundaries of areas. According to the previous theory, the geographic extent of the job market is a direct function of skill. Thus moves between large areas should represent the effects of job markets for the highly skilled more than moves within large areas. The geographical extent of the housing market, besides lying within a commuting ring for a given job location, depends upon the heterogeneity of housing and of neighborhoods within these rings. Thus the size and boundaries of small areas may obscure the influence of the housing market by obscuring the heterogeneity of the areas.

There are three points made in the classic research literature: (1) Net migration can be interpreted as an effort to increase economic opportunity. (2) The volume of migration between pairs of cities stands in some direct relation to the populations of the two cities (perhaps a linear relation to the product of the two populations) and in some inverse relation to the distance between the cities (perhaps a linear relation to the square of the distance). (3) There is a marked difference in the age and sex characteristics of migration streams between different types of areas. The literature is well summarized in Isard's *Methods of Regional Analysis*,[6] and in Shryock's *Population Mobility Within the United States*.[7]

These three classical points are ordinarily presented by summary descriptions of migration data without attempting to derive any one of them from a social theory, let alone the possibility of demonstrating that all of them are the consequences of a single social theory. Yet the theoretical structure laid out at the beginning of this chapter implies all three points, and many more besides. We must note that these studies defined migration as moves between cities, or even larger regions, so that the household life-cycle variables of our theory cannot be tested—only the job-related variables.

We next note that, if we consider job opportunities to be the driving mechanism of migration, there is a clear-cut utility interpretation of all three classical findings. Statement (1) is the crudest possible deduction from any such theory; statement (2) follows if job opportunities are proportional to total population but knowledge of job opportunities decreases with distance between cities; and (3) follows if job opportunities are differentiated by age, sex, and other social characteristics.

The argument above is similar to that of Stouffer.[8] He argues that, for a given distribution of opportunities, migration would tend to minimize distance (apparently he has cost in mind as an explanation for distance, but he also considers knowledge of available opportunities). But the definition of an opportunity is disaggregated— that is, not uniform over a given population. Thus the minimization should occur within income groups and within racial groups for short-distance moves (housing shifts within a large city) or within occupational groups for long-distance moves involving job opportunities. This amounts to saying that the significance of distance is constrained by the social characteristics of the decision maker and by the distributions of "vacancies" over areas. The latter point is equivalent to a description of markets —that is, a "vacancy" is necessarily the result of (1) a utility comparison by a decision maker, and (2) the workings of market mechanisms over large areas. Note that Stouffer's differentiation of the theoretical factors in short-distance (housing-related) moves and in long-distance (job-related) moves is entirely compatible with the theoretical argument given in the first part of this chapter.

Unfortunately very little research was undertaken that could be considered as a direct test of this theory, although a number of related pieces of research supported its plausibility. Distance minimization for disaggregated populations was revealed by Stouffer himself, by Dorothy S. Thomas,[9] and by others.[10] But the measurement of opportunities was so poor that one could not assert that the theory was verified, especially in its social-psychological detail.

We can, however, throw more light on this type of argument with recent research. Let us first consider the influence of job opportunities upon long-distance moves. Here we can turn to census data that relate occupations to migration streams over a set of areas, and to social-psychological studies that relate job choice to area choice. Studies of the former were made by Nishiura, using census tabulations on migration streams in Indiana.[11] Studies of the second type were directed by the author and by Vernon W. Ruttan at Purdue University, including work by Olson, Geschwind, Cohen, and Schuh, using three rural community studies in Indiana that made social-psychological and economic measures of individuals possible.[12]

The overall significance of the Indiana studies is that they support the following theoretical notions. Long-distance moves imply change of job. Change of job is associated with transfer of assets, skill, and business property. Transfer of assets is associated with market conditions. In the matter of skills alone, the market conditions turn on (1) The differential availability of job opportunities, by area and by skill; (2) The extent of diffusion of knowledge of job opportunities, by area and by skill; and (3) The career constraints on entry into and retention of a given skill category—i.e., occupation prerequisites, by education and by age. For business property alone, market conditions turn on the salability of present property, largely determined by local business conditions, plus the availability of alternative properties that provide at least equivalent returns. Both types of transfer of assets are represented by the independent doctor, dentist, or lawyer, but for most other occupations there is a fairly clear distinction between one or the other type of transfer. That is, most entrepreneurs have few specific skills, while most skilled persons do not own their own business.

Long-distance moves also imply change of residence. Costs of change of residence are associated with distance of move and quantity of persons and of household goods to be moved. The quantity of persons and of household goods ordinarily increases from marriage until children start to leave home, then decreases.

Thus the distance between areas, and the age of the persons, influence both job change and residence change, but in different ways. In general we expect the number of moves to decline as distance between areas increases, and we expect the number of moves to decline as age of persons increases, but there are important qualifications in the theoretical argument stated above. Skill and market conditions can offset these generalizations. In particular we expect that high skill will tend to offset both distance and age, and that the magnitude of this effect will depend on differential growth of job opportunities by area.

Consider first the findings from census data. The differential growth of job opportunities has been most marked in the contrast of rural and urban areas. Therefore we should expect that rural-urban migration streams would reveal the influence of transfer of assets upon different occupations. Thus when we see that the professionals are first in all long-distance moves, that higher education has a pronounced effect for all streams with rural origins or urban destinations (the most extreme education influence being observed in the rural-urban streams), the skill aspect of our argument can be considered sustained. We can further note that if job opportunities are declining in an area, the possibility of selling a business is also declining relative to the possibility for sale if job opportunities are not declining. The data show that proprietors were second only to professionals in all streams with urban origins, but were last in the rural-urban streams and the rural-suburban streams.

The three community studies give further support to these arguments. They were rural communities similar in size and population but with very different economic parameters. One was a commercial center for a highly prosperous agricultural area; one a commercial center for a drastically declining agricultural area. The third was a commercial center for a moderately prosperous agricultural area but, more important, was the only one sufficiently close to a metropolitan area to share in its growth and expansion. Although preachers and teachers were highly mobile in all of the communities, entrepreneurs were trapped in the drastically declining community, were satisfied with the prosperous community, and could and did sell when convenient in the metropolitan fringe community—both store owners and farm owners. The educational and age characteristics of the communities reflect the influence of these migration processes. The young and the skilled have departed from the declining community, inheritance of farms and businesses characterizes the prosperous community leading to an even age distribution associated with high education, and an intermediate pattern is revealed for the other community.

The Nishiura study was an effort to test theories of the type proposed by Sara Smith Sutker[13] with research of the type carried out by Dorothy Swaine Thomas, Warren Thompson, Donald Bogue, and Margaret Hagood.[14] The previous research in this tradition had noted the differential characteristics of the various types of migration streams, as we have noted above. The four persons mentioned above had carried out studies that attempted to consider several social variables simultaneously rather than appraising their separate effects. This tradition reached its zenith in the study by Bogue and Hagood called *Differential Migration in the Corn and Cotton Belts.* The volume of data summarized in these studies is so enormous that it defies interpretation—other than to note that the discussion above is more or less substantiated.

The Nishiura study thus began with a summary and interpretation of the empirical generalizations presented by previous researchers, then demonstrated that this interpretation was further substantiated by another set of tabulations. In these tabulations the characteristics of the streams were standardized by the characteristics of areas of origin. Thus the characteristics of the streams can be interpreted from the decision-theory vantage point used above.

The same notions of decision theory can be used in the interpretation of migration within a metropolitan area. We have, however, two differences. First, the set of variables and the theories that specify relations among variables are quite different. Second, there is very little research on the streams of migration for such areas. A little has been done on the decision to move, but without tracing the location of the new residence, while a lot has been done on describing the distribution of the social characteristics of areas at any given census, especially in terms of segregation;[15] but between the decision to move and the distribution that results as an aggregate over many such decisions and their outcomes there is much room for further empirical work.

Let us suppose that, within a metropolitan area, the response to household pressures for moving is determined by the expected future income, transferability of residential assets, family life-cycle changes, and the social-status aspirations. Let us assume that all households initially rent, but that aspirations for social status yield a continuous pressure for home ownership, subject to income constraints. Changes of residence without changes of job, without shifting to ownership, and without increasing income, should be primarily in response to life-cycle changes. Changes to ownership will largely be determined by increased expected future income. Changes from ownership to ownership will be constrained by expected future income in combination with the salability of property; within these limits life-cycle changes and social-status aspirations will determine moves. Changes from ownership to rental will largely reflect life-cycle changes, e.g., contracting family size.

Two studies throw very partial light on these processes. A study by Rossi sought to identify dissatisfaction with housing in a Philadelphia sample, and therefore predict likelihood for moving from a particular housing unit.[16] His results emphasized the importance of life-cycle changes as an impetus to moving. A study by Leslie and Richardson, using similar research techniques upon a prefabricated housing development in Lafayette, Indiana, throws light upon the moves of owners.[17] In these results the movers were largely those persons with higher skills and rapidly increasing expected future incomes; they were younger than nonmovers. In contrast the nonmovers had very flat, though stable, future-income curves. Life-cycle variables had little relation to moving.

A great many studies attest to the presence of pronounced segregation of urban populations, and to the preservation of segregation through patterns of residential change.[18] These studies may be viewed as support for the importance of social-status aspirations as described above.

In summary, then, we have attempted to interpret the migration research literature from the same theoretical perspective that we used for the fertility research literature. In migration, household decision making is different from that in fertility. The joint decision of husband and wife is different. We also note the significance of markets as constraints on migration decisions, especially job markets and housing markets. We hope that the general theoretical argument is illuminated by the contrast of migration and fertility. Needless to say, we also hope that the migration-research literature is also illuminated by our interpretation.

NOTES

1. See Walter Isard, *Methods of Regional Analysis* (New York: Wiley, 1960), Chap. 3; see also Dorothy S. Thomas, *Research Memorandum on Migration Differentials* (New York: Social Science Research Council, 1938).

2. John S. McDonald and Leatrice D. McDonald, "Chain Migration, Ethnic Neighborhood Formation and Social Networks," *Milbank Memorial Fund Quarterly*, LXII, No. 1 (January 1964), 82–91.

3. W. I. Thomas and Florian Znaniecki, *The Polish Peasant in Europe and America* (2 vols.; New York: Knopf, 1927); C. Wright Mills, Clarence Senior, and Rose Kohn Goldsen, *The Puerto Rican Journey* (New York: Harper, 1960); James S. Brown, Harry Schwarzweller, and Joseph J. Mangalam, "Kentucky Mountain Migration and the Stem Family: An American Variation on a Theme by Le Play," *Rural Society*, XXVIII (March 1963), 48–9.

4. Herbert J. Gans, *The Urban Villagers* (New York: Free Press, 1962); William F. Whyte, *Street Corner Society* (Chicago, Ill.: U. of Chicago Press, 1942, 1955).

5. See Charles Abrams, *Man's Struggle for Shelter in an Urbanizing World* (Cambridge, Mass.: M.I.T. Press, 1964), Chap. 2.

6. Isard, *op. cit.*

7. Henry S. Shyrock, Jr., *Population Mobility within the United States* (Chicago, Ill.: Community and Family Study Center, U. of Chicago, 1964).

8. Samuel A. Stouffer, "Intervening Opportunities: A Theory Relating Mobility and Distance," *American Sociological Review*, V (1940), 845–67. See also his recent collection of articles, *Social Research to Test Ideas* (New York: Free Press, 1962), Chap. 4.

9. Dorothy S. Thomas and Margaret Bright, "Interstate Migration and Intervening Opportunities," *American Sociological Review*, VI, 773–83.

10. See Isard, *op. cit.*, Chap. 11.

11. Eleanor N. Nishiura, *Internal Migration in Indiana*, Ph.D. thesis, Purdue University, August 1959; James M. Beshers and Eleanor N. Nishiura, "A Theory of Internal Migration Differentials," *Social Forces*, XXXIX (1961), 214–18.

12. Philip G. Olson, "Job Mobility and Migration in a High Income Rural Community," Purdue Agricultural Experiment Station Bulletin 708 (1960); R. D. Geschwind and Vernon W. Ruttan, "Job Mobility and Migration in a Low Income Rural Community," Purdue Agricultural Experiment Station Bulletin 730 (1961); Lois K. Cohen and G. Edward Schuh, "Job Mobility and Migration in a Middle Income Small Town with Comparisons to High and Low Income Communities," Purdue Agricultural Experiment Station Bulletin 763 (1963).

13. Sara Smith (Sutker), *The Occupational System and Migration within the United States: A Sociological Reconceptualization of a Demographic Problem*, Ph.D. thesis, University of North Carolina, 1955.

14. See, for example, Thomas and Bright, *op. cit.*; Warren S. Thompson, *Migration Within Ohio, 1935–40* (Oxford, Ohio: Scripps Foundation, 1951); Donald J. Bogue and Margaret Jarman Hagood, *Differential Migration in the Corn and Cotton Belts* (Oxford, Ohio: Scripps Foundation, 1953).

15. See, for example, Otis Dudley Duncan and Beverly Duncan, "Residential Distribution and Occupational Stratification," *American Journal of Sociology*, LX (March 1955), 493, reprinted in Paul K. Hatt and Albert J. Reiss, Jr. (eds.), *Cities and Society* (New York: Free Press, 1957); Otis Dudley Duncan and Beverly Duncan, *The Negro Population of Chicago* (Chicago, Ill.: U. of Chicago Press, 1957); Otis Dudley Duncan and Stanley Lieberson, "Ethnic Segregation and Assimilation," *American Journal of Sociology*, LXIV (January 1959), 364–74; Stanley Lieberson, *Ethnic Patterns in American Cities* (New York: Free Press, 1963).

16. Peter Rossi, *Why Families Move* (New York: Free Press, 1955).

17. Gerald R. Leslie and Arthur H. Richardson, "Life Cycle, Career Pattern, and Decision to Move," *American Sociological Review*, XXVI (December 1961), 894–902.

18. See Edgar C. Rust III, *Intra-Metropolitan Migration: Six Boston Area Municipalities*, M.C.P. thesis, Massachusetts Institute of Technology, June 1963, for evidence on the relationship between migration and segregation.

CHAPTER 6

Mortality

IN our discussion of mortality in Chapter 2 we noted
that the diffusion of new technology was the most
obvious factor in the decline of mortality during the
Demographic Transition. The diffusion of this technology has many interesting social facets; in part it results
from public-health activities that may modify the environment as in the control of typhus, malaria, or ty-
phoid fever, or may involve such social actions as mass
diagnosis (TB x-ray), mass treatment (smallpox inocu-
lation), or quarantine (infectious diseases). In part it
stems from the family decision to seek medical services.

There are four major social aspects of the decline in
mortality. The first is in the implications of the technol-

(153)

ogy itself—the great infectious diseases have steadily come under control, to the extent that in the West they have been replaced as leading causes of mortality by the degenerative diseases. In particular, infant mortality and the mortality of women due to childbearing have both been greatly reduced. The enormous increases in population growth that resulted from these changes have been discussed in Chapter 2. But we must also note that the age and sex distribution of the population shifted dramatically, that the composition of households changed, and that the makeup of the labor force altered also. Further we must note that reduction of mortality did not necessarily imply the elimination of ill health. Thus today attention has shifted to the social costs of disease other than the costs of death itself. These costs include labor-force implications as well as the costs of the medical services for partially debilitating diseases.

The changes noted above have come with different pace to different nations, different regions within nations (urban and rural especially), and different occupations. The timing, in general, represents differential access to medical services favoring higher-ranking occupations and urban residents, but is also influenced by the differential distribution of infectious conditions (concentrated in cities) and the specific public-health measures that may have contributed to the control of these conditions. There are also special environmental implications of occupations that enter in—for example, mining and silicosis.

Evidence of the diffusion of medical technology can be found in the convergence of many measures of mortality by nation, region, race, and occupation. These differentials are influenced by the organization of medical services and by the form of public-health programs. For infectious diseases the distribution of contacts within the population influences the spread of illness, contagion. Since the distribution of contacts is strongly affected by population density and segregation (of races, occupations, religions) there should initially be large differentials that may be widened before they converge. Occupation also serves as an index of income and of attitudes toward medical services, thus influencing the likelihood that an individual or family will make use of these services. As average personal income increases and as favorable attitudes toward medical services diffuse, greater use is made of medical services and health differentials should decline.

Note that the existence of differentials of mortality among segments of the population was the starting place for epidemiology.

Even after the main impact of the new medical tech-

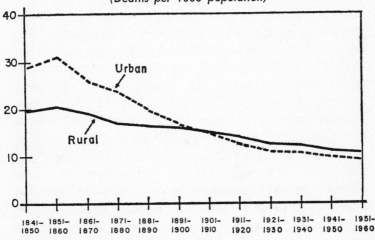

Figure 6–1
Sweden: Urban and Rural Death Rates, 1841–1900
(Deaths per 1000 population)

Source: Štatistik Arsbok för Sverige, 1951 and 1963.

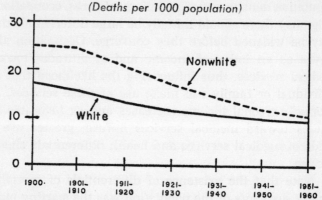

Figure 6-2

United States: White and Nonwhite Death Rates, 1900-1960
(Deaths per 1000 population)

Source: U.S. National office of Vital Statistics, *Vital Statistics of the United States, 1961,* Vol. II, Mortality, Part A (Washington, D.C., Public Health Service, 1964), Table 1-1. 1900-1932 rates are for death registration states only.

nology has been felt there remain some residual puzzles, especially in the differential incidence of certain diseases by region, occupations, and sex. It is quite difficult to sort out the influences of biological, environmental, and social variables in susceptibility to these diseases. Explanations that treat tension or mental illness as major components of these illnesses are particularly difficult to evaluate. The symptoms of mental illness are often intertwined with those of physical illness. For any given individual different symptoms at different times may reflect a single illness. Many individuals with similar symptoms apparently have different illnesses, while individuals with unlike symptoms may turn out to have the same illness. The cultural influences upon symptom selection also appear to be large—there seem to be socially acceptable symptoms of mental illness at any time, such as classical hysteria described by Freud, and there seem to be fashions influencing change of these socially acceptable symptoms—the patient's report and the doctor's diagnosis being so influenced.

A study of mortality differentials by sex provides a perspective on the stress hypothesis. Madigan posed the possibility of contrasting mortality rates for sex within similar occupations.[1] In particular, he noted that the teaching orders of the Catholic Church impose obligations upon their members that do not differentiate greatly by sex. Thus the possibility existed of collecting death records from these teaching orders.

The phenomenon on which Madigan sought to throw light was the increasing differential in life expectancy by sex in this century. Following the decline in death from childbirth, female life expectancy steadily increased. But the surprise was that the increase for females was substantially more rapid than that for males, leading to a great surplus of females in the older age groups. Explanations of two kinds were put forward, one focusing on the occupational hazards of males, the other on the innate biological strength of females that presumably stemmed from the demands of childbearing upon genetic selection.

The former approach led to a detailed consideration of sex differences in specific causes of death, with heart disease attracting much attention. Occupational stress of a psychological nature was often suggested. The latter approach led to a consideration of female physiology and metabolism from the point of view of resistance to illness. Data showing that prior to puberty male mortality greatly exceeded female mortality, and that before birth the female fetus had a greater chance of survival than the male fetus, seemed to support the second line of investigation. One should note that both kinds of factors could well be operating, but there was some interest in trying to determine the relative importance of these factors.

The data assembled by Madigan reveal two phenomena clearly. For both sexes length of life within the teaching orders was increasing more rapidly than in the general population. There was, however, a clear opening of the gap between the sexes; within this special population the length of life of females relative to the length of life of males was increasing even faster than in the general population. It appears that, with occupation held constant, a strong biological factor favoring females is revealed.

A qualifying argument can be made against these data. One can say that occupation was held constant at a very low level of occupational stress. Perhaps differential sex mortality for occupations of characteristically high stress should be determined, especially those occupations that appear linked to heart disease and ulcers.

Another dimension to the interpretation stems from the extremely rapid increase of life expectancy among the young Sisters. In regard to this finding Madigan "suggests the hypothesis that *under conditions of equal stress* women may be no more resistant to the *infectious* and *contagious* diseases than men—perhaps even less so— and that the gains which women have been making over men in this century may be chiefly bound up with a greater constitutional resistance to the *degenerative* diseases."[2]

The recent trends in mortality in the West cast a little light, but also much darkness, upon the relative significance of the degenerative diseases and the stress hypotheses. Perhaps the best approach is to summarize recent discussions of disease specific mortality trends by Mori-yama[3] and by Spiegelman.[4] Moriyama presents an overall picture of recent trends in U.S. mortality. He demonstrates that mortality leveled off, or even slightly increased, in the 1950's following a period of rapid decline from the 1930's. He presents a detailed tabulation of mortality by age, by sex, by color and by cause in the U.S. from the 1930's to 1960 (different causes have different initial dates). Moriyama summarizes these data in the following way:

This study indicates that the leveling off of the death rates can be accounted for by the combination of two sets of factors. The first is the dramatic drop in death rate for the diseases of infectious origin with the successive introduction and application of pneumonia serum therapy, the sulfa drugs, and the antibiotics. The accelerated decline started about 1938 and then lost its impetus in the 1950's. By that time, the mortality from diseases of infectious origin had reached a level where it no longer contributed in a major way to the total number of deaths. Even if the trend of the death rates for the infective and parasitic diseases, including pneumonia and influenza, had continued downward without interruption, this would not have accounted for all of the leveling off of the total death rate.

However, the long-term decline in mortality from the infectious diseases resulted in a major realignment of the principal causes of death which uncovered a second set of factors. These factors involve the trends of mortality from the presently numerically important causes of death, namely, malignant neoplasms and cardiovascular-renal diseases at all ages, congenital malformations through the childhood years, accidents and other violence from childhood through middle age, cirrhosis of the liver, in middle age, and diabetes mellitus from middle age into old age. Also, new problems are emerging. The dramatic upward trend of the chronic bronchopulmonary disease mortality from middle age onward seems particularly significant. None of the trends for these causes of death exhibits the same rate of decline as the trend for the infective diseases. In fact, many of the trends are rising by different degrees. The combined effect of these various trends is to slow down the rate of decline of the total death rate.[5]

Moriyama further argues that the chronic diseases, accidents, and other violence are the most important factors in the leveling off of death rates. Even so, only the elimination of cardiovascular disease, among specific causes of death, would result in large increases in life expectancy. Among special factors Moriyama notes that "Cirrhosis of the liver has already come to the forefront as one of the five principal causes of death in the age groups 35–54 years, and the death rate for this disease is still increasing rapidly."[6] Since this latter disease is associated with excessive consumption of alcohol we might view it as a consequence of psychological stress or tension. Such a psychological component might be present in deaths from cardiovascular disease, accidents, and other violence.

Spiegelman presents annual death rates by cause (but not by age or sex) for twenty "countries of low mortality," 1950–61. A general pattern of similarity among countries emerges, though not without many puzzles. We quote here his Conclusion.

A more detailed insight into trends of death rates for specific causes in countries of low mortality would necessarily require study according to age and sex. The surface indications furnished by an examination of crude death rates since 1950 in the countries of western Europe and English-speaking countries elsewhere show that the rate of reduction in mortality from 1950–53 to 1954–57 did not continue into the period 1958–61 for many nations. Although the major element in this situation appears to be the cardiovascular-renal diseases, the failure to show improvement, either by a reduction in mortality or by a lessening rate of increase, was shared by influenza and pneumonia.

Within the broad categories of causes of death—such as the cardiovascular-renal diseases, cancer, and accidents—the more specific conditions or injuries may not show parallel trends; some may indeed be contrary. Ordinarily, it would be expected that the trend patterns for these more specific conditions or injuries would be similar in countries of low mortality, since they have ample opportunity for ready communication of advances in medical knowledge and practice.[7]

These data lend some support to both degenerative and stress hypotheses, but in particular they point out the possibility of overlap, or of multiple causation. The influence of smoking and alcohol, for example, may stem from a desire to control tension and stress, but then lead to intensification of the degenerative processes. Accidents, violence, and suicide all involve stress components at the individual level as well as social factors that influence both the occurrence of stress and the manifestation of stress.

Many sociologists believe that individual stress can be absorbed by the emotional supports of groups. Thus, for example, life expectancy should be longer for married persons than for single, widowed, or divorced persons. Durkheim worked out the argument in some detail in his analysis of suicide, yet he clearly indicated that other causes of death could be derived from his general argument.[8] The fugitive data available for total mortality do support this view. Further research on the point would be most welcome.

In recent years the environment has been viewed as a source of increasing mortality, as in the discussion of air pollution. Sorting out this influence statistically would be an extremely difficult task. A special problem is raised by radioactive fallout because its lethal influence may be genetically transferred to future generations. Human biologists have begun the appropriate research to estimate this influence. In doing so they have had to gain much skill in handling social data and social variables.

There is the further genetic possibility of the effects upon selection itself of these changing patterns of mortality. Not only are certain types of people more likely to live to maturity than before, but they are also more likely to transmit genes to future generations. Although the students of eugenics make clear the possibilities that might result, we have here another case in which evidence is extremely difficult to collect.

In summary, much significant social research could be carried out on health and mortality. In particular, the sorting out of the causality of social and of biological factors would be most enlightening.

NOTES

1. See Rupert B. Vance and Francis C. Madigan, S.J., "Differential Mortality and the 'Style of Life' of Men and Women: a Research Design," *Trends and Differentials in Mortality* (New York: Milbank Memorial Fund, 1955), 150–63; Francis C. Madigan, S.J. and Rupert B. Vance, "Differential Sex Mortality: A Research Design," *Social Forces*, XXXV, No. 3 (March 1957), 193–9; Francis C. Madigan, S.J., "Are Sex Mortality Differences Biologically Caused?" *Milbank Memorial Fund Quarterly*, XXXV, No. 2 (April 1957), 202–23.

2. Madigan, *op. cit.* (April 1957), pp. 20–1.

3. U. S. National Center for Health Statistics, "The Change in Mortality Trends in the United States," Washington, D.C.: U. S. Department of Health, Education and Welfare, Public Health Service, 1964. Report prepared by Iwao M. Moriyama.

4. Mortimer Spiegelman, "Mortality Trends for Causes of Death in Countries of Low Mortality," *Demography*, II (1965), 115–25.

5. U. S. National Center for Health Statistics, *op. cit.*, pp. 37–8.

6. *Ibid.*, p. 38.

7. Spiegelman, *op. cit.*, pp. 124–25.

8. Emile Durkheim, *Suicide*, trans. by J. A. Spaulding and George Simpson (New York: Free Press, 1962).

CHAPTER 7

The Impact of Population
Processes on Social Systems

I N previous chapters we have elaborated a theory of
the influence of social variables upon population
processes—births, deaths, and migration. Now we
must consider the other side of the relationship, the influence of population processes on social variables. Note
the circularity of these influences—a desirable circularity. Until now we have treated the social variables as
given, but if knowledge of the population processes
enabled us to predict the state of the social variables we
would have a more complete theory, one capable of yielding much more interesting predictions. (Needless to say,

(163)

we do not expect to obtain a completely circular deterministic theory.)

There are two parts to this problem. First, we must specify the links between the population processes and the social variables such that a change in the former will induce a change in the latter; we must not only name the links, we must also state the explicit relationships that permit prediction. Second, we must note the consequences of the changes of the social variables—the consequences at the level of the social system within which these processes are taking place.

Both parts are well illustrated by the argument of Malthus. The links occur in the ratio of population increase to resources increase—the trend in per capita resources. The consequences are the rising indices of social breakdown—war, famine, disease, and crime—which come into play long before the rise in death rates can restore an equilibrium.

Let us elaborate both of these points in Malthus and in other more recent writers. First consider the links from population processes to social systems. The classic position is that increase in population tends toward a decrease in per capita resources. For Malthus the crucial definition of resources was food. He argued that, in general, the growth of human population would tend to exceed the growth of food. Since the growth of humans and of food are both biological processes, one might assume that they are governed by the same laws of growth, and that influence of technology upon agriculture might lead to a greater growth rate than that of the human population. But Malthus believed that the productive capacity of land was limited, that intitially land of high productivity and with a great rate of response to technology might be cultivated, but that the need for food would lead to the cultivation of marginal lands with low productivity and little response to technology.

In the recent history of the West two aspects of Malthus' argument have not been vindicated, both arising from technology. The impact of birth-control technology on human population growth rates has led to far lower rates of growth than had previously been expected. The impact of chemistry and of mechanization on agriculture has led to food-production rates far higher than expected. For those parts of the world that have not yet passed into the third stage of the demographic transition, however, the Malthusian dilemma is a very vivid phenomenon.

As an alternative we may define resources as wealth, as in a gross national product, and relate population growth to per capita wealth. This is the case, for example, with the Five-Year Plans of India. The influence of technology upon industrial production is taken into account in per capita wealth. While population growth directly affects the denominator of wealth per capita, it may also affect the numerator. To determine the influence of population growth on wealth we need to know about systems of production and systems of distribution. On one hand we must know more about the capital investment in technology, the organization of industry, and the skills of the population; on the other, we must know more about the systems for marketing, transportation, finance, and credit. The per capita productivity of nations varies greatly according to the former; the per capita demand varies according to the latter. For certain commodities in some societies it has been argued (for example by Kuznets[1]) that an increasing population yields increased demand which will in turn lead to increased investment in technology, which in turn finally leads to increased productivity per capita.

This argument may be valid in certain situations; to determine its limits we would like to separate two ways in which change in markets might increase demand, the structural change of markets by transportation and packaging technology, and the increase of markets due to population growth. We would also like to compare markets in those societies in which investment is sensitive to consumer demand with markets in those societies in which investment is controlled by other considerations—perhaps a socialist economy.

It is also possible that fluctuations in per capita wealth could lead to fluctuations in population, with a suitable lagged effect. Certainly this is the implication of the argument in Chapter 4 for the fertility behavior of family planners. Such adjustments of population to wealth would have different implications of population growth for per capita wealth from those situations in which population growth is insensitive to wealth.

The same reservations must be expressed for a variant of Malthus' position which appears in classical economics —the theory of optimum population.[2] This theory holds that for a given economic system there will be an optimum population size consistent with the best performance of the system, and any variation of the population size away from this optimum, either more or less, will result in economic loss, or cost. This argument is an excellent example of the use of mathematical methods in economics that are not relevant.

If one sets up a system of equations to define an economic system, with population size as one of the parameters, and with a criterion variable that is to be maximized, then one can solve the equations in such a way as to obtain a relation between population size and the other parameters consistent with the maximum value of the criterion variable. Then if one further specifies absolute values for all the other parameters and the constants he also specifies an absolute value for population size. But there are two major shortcomings to this procedure.

First, there are alternative equations that are equally useful—for example, equations with population growth rather than population size as a parameter, or equations that attempt to reflect changes in technology or economic structure in the choice of parameters. Solving such equations would produce an optimum trajectory of population growth in relation to the trajectories of the other parameters. In special cases it might turn out that the optimum trajectory of population growth is zero, independent of the values of the other parameters, but it is hardly likely that this would be the general or typical solution.

Second, the notion of a single well-defined optimum is not very defensible in problems of this type. Gunnar Myrdal pointed out that a curve relating population size to some measure of performance of an economy was not likely to rise to a sharp peak at a single population size, say 1,607,382, but was more likely to resemble a bread-loaf, with extremely small or extremely large populations having a marked negative effect upon economic performance, but with intermediate population sizes having little systematic relation to economic performance.[3]

We have now described the link from population processes to social systems as it was posed by Malthus and modified by his successors. This argument is couched in economic terms. But the implications of population growth were much more broadly conceived by Malthus. He argued that the decline of per capita resources would ultimately lead to an increase in death rates, which would restore an equilibrium between population and resources.

Prior to the actual increase of death rates, however, he prophesied a rather general social breakdown; war, famine, crime, and disease would bring increasing social costs long before equilibrium was restored. Note that these are general social conditions, characteristics of social systems rather than characteristics of individuals. Less thoughtful social scientists can only perceive effects upon individuals, or personality.

Besides Malthus many other persons have written on the influence of population upon social systems. They vary by the links proposed between population and social variables, and by the consequences that they predict upon social systems. The influence of population has been ascribed to the total number of people in an area and the density of population per area, as well as total population growth that we have discussed above. The consequences of the total number of people have been expressed in terms of military power of nations and in terms of resulting forms of social organization (Simmel).[4] The consequences of population density have been described in terms of mental illness and in terms of the pathology of social organization—Durkheim's concept of moral density,[5] Meier's concern for urban information overload,[6] and Calhoun's animal experiments on high density[7] are all part of this discussion.

In contrast to other social scientists, the professional demographers have focused their attention on the rates of demographic changes. These underlying rates determine the total population size, the density, and the total growth rate; thus no generality is lost with this apparent narrowing of the problem. The effects of rates of demographic changes go beyond the growth of total population; births, deaths, and migration determine the age, sex, and geographical distribution of the population; in addition, they are social events with significance in their own right. The differential growth of segments of the population has implications for shifts of power within social systems, especially political systems that operate under voting rules, as well as for the allocation or distribution of commodities.

In this book we have extended the traditional concern for predicting rates of demographic changes to a more detailed consideration of social variables. Thus we have raised the possibility of predicting differential population growth from social variables. Now we would like to state the reciprocal influence of population processes upon social variables. In particular we hope to express the influence of population processes upon social structure through market notions. A market is normally conceived of as a set of commodities flowing among persons. Suppose we change the number of persons in order to view the impact upon the flow of commodities. This amounts to adjusting demand in classical economics. Thus we see that the demand for commodities is in part the supply of persons. A market is then viewed as an interaction between a supply of commodities and a supply of persons.

In order to develop this thought we must recall our previous argument. Social variables influence population through household decision processes. Constraints upon household decision processes include age, occupation, income, education, and so on. In order to take account of social change we have used cohort notions—that is, we have tried to keep track of different generations as well as of age in our analysis.

What we then viewed as constraints on decision processes we now view as variables. These variables will respond to population processes through the operation of markets. Two aspects of these market mechanisms must be carefully specified—the time lags and the level of aggregation.

The difficult market concepts have already been illustrated with the discussion of migration in Chapter 5. We have to consider the supply of population as the source of demand for the supply of jobs and of housing, thus variations in the supply of population will influence the markets for jobs and for housing. One can argue for the existence of market adjustment of the supply of population both through migration and through births, but the lag in response of reduction of births upon the job market is so great that the notion of an adjustment is rather tenuous.

The geographical extent of a market is also a part of the aggregation problem. Again we saw this with migration. The extent of job markets differed according to the skills of the workers. The extent of housing markets is influenced by commuting patterns.

Another illustration of difficulties with market notions comes from the study of marriage markets—supplies and demands for mates. In this instance the distribution of marriages itself affects the transmission of social characteristics to future generations, while the distribution of marriages will be influenced by the social characteristics of the eligible mates.[8] In terms of the makeup of the social stratification system these are extremely significant effects, yet they operate with long time lags, and thus are often ignored.

Perhaps these difficult theoretical issues can be clarified by an abstract representation of the problem. We shall use the metaphor of flows over a network. The network can be described as a set of nodes between each pair of which flows can be defined. Frequently we will be interested in the case of directed flows between pairs of nodes. Thus there will be two possible flows between each pair of nodes, and asymmetric flows (as in one-way streets) will be allowed.

These metaphors can be used to define networks in which the nodes represent persons and the flows indicate various interchanges among persons—interchanges of economic commodities for example. It is also useful to define networks in which the nodes represent sets of persons and the flows are persons moving from node to node—migration among areas for example. The relations between these two networks must be brought out.

First of all we must note that the distinction between nodes and flows is of practical utility if the rate of change of nodes is very slow relative to the rate of change of flows. Thus the nodes define the relatively stable reference axes in terms of which we can describe the flows. If the flows are represented in time units such as days or weeks, such as consumer purchases, then the designation of persons as nodes may be justified on the grounds that births and deaths of individuals are relatively rare events within a few weeks, or even within a year. If, however, we extend our time span, the assumption of negligible influence for births and deaths may no longer be warranted. From this perspective the problem here is to express the influence of birth and death processes of the nodes upon the flows among the nodes. In particular we would like to know if the slower changes introduce strong constraints on the faster changes—the flows.

This view of things, the concern for rates of change in the definition of the reference axes themselves, is not commonly adopted. There is another more obvious relation between these two kinds of networks. This is the implication that the network with persons as nodes has for the network with sets of persons as nodes. It is possible, by definition, to aggregate over any network of the former type to obtain a network of the latter type. Thus if we are given some propositions describing flows over the former network, then we can deduce the consequences for various networks of the latter kind. By performing aggregations of this type we are allowing ourselves to study certain net effects of the flows, or transactions. For example, if we aggregate individuals into households we can examine the net consumption for the household as a unit.

The classic market concept is useful in describing the dependencies of these flows. Here we have a set of commodities flowing among persons (with a reverse flow of money). There is a supply of commodities in a given time period. Further, the demand for commodities is defined over the set of persons, or nodes. Suppose for each person the preference for a commodity is reduced to two alternatives, yes or no. In this case we have defined the relevant supply of persons as a subset of the total set of persons represented in the network. In general, demand for commodities can be interpreted as a description of the relevant supply of persons. If we introduce births and deaths of persons into such networks then it is clear that we must specify the demand implications of these births and deaths. If we adequately specify these demand implications then we have solved the problem of representing the influence of change in the reference axes upon change in the flows for this particular commodity and set of persons. In other words, we must relate propositions of the distribution of commodities to propositions of the distribution of persons. Economists have used the utility concept for this purpose.

Let us now consider how to represent social mobility with these networks. The problem differs according to the social characteristics with respect to which people may be changing. Some social characteristics, such as income, may fluctuate drastically within short time periods, say a year, while other characteristics, such as race, may fluctuate much less. Even for income, however, we may choose to neglect short-term fluctuations. Further, if we define nodes of the network as income categories we can represent income change as flows of persons rather than flows of money.

Suppose we take the generation as a time unit for representing social mobility. This is the longest time lag in the transmission of social characteristics from parent to child, to the extent that the previous history is articulated through the parent. Genetic flows occur at generation lengths, and behavior acquired in childhood can occur only once in a generation. Further, with the generation as a time period we can link associate births; for example, the birth of a female can be related to the later births of her offspring.

Given the generation as a time unit, marriage must be represented. In a previous book I have developed an elaborate argument on the relation between marriage, social mobility, and the system of stratification. That argument, however, did not take account of the influences of differential birth and marriage rates upon social mobility.

It is clear that a notion of a marriage market and of utility functions can be used in this problem. Since status symbols play the role of a generalized commodity we must have their supply characteristics adequately represented, i.e., the production of symbols and of persons stands in demand and supply relations. If we regard the absolute number of status symbols as fixed, then an increase in population should yield an increase in the utility of the status symbol; the latter would have become a relatively scarce resource. If we regard the proportional distribution of status symbols as fixed, then we can disregard total population growth, but we must keep an eye on differential growth. (In relation to occupations, such dynamics have been discussed by Elbridge Sibley,[9] and by Davis and Moore.[10] The supply of occupations and of persons can be related to the net mobility that must occur as a minimum, and to the utility of occupations in terms of relative scarcity.)

Suppose the utility function governing mate selection gives highest value to a person of similar social characteristics, say the same religion (a view widely held among marriage sociologists). Then satisfaction in part depends upon the available supply of persons of the same religion, say in the same region. If in the queueing and matching process this criterion cannot be satisfied, then one must either marry outside the preferred group or not marry at all. Either alternative has substantial consequences for the stratification system in the next generation. The first alternative tends to blur the distinction in the population, while the second tends to eliminate the group in the long run and to reduce its political influence in the short run.

Canadian census data on religious intermarriage have been examined by Heer.[11] He is able to demonstrate that the supply of mates influences patterns of intermarriage by comparing Canadian cities with quite different religious compositions.

Another type of utility function has been described by anthropologists. They have collected elaborate information on the marriage rules in primitive societies. Marion Levy and his colleagues have demonstrated that, under reasonable assumptions of birth and death rates in these societies, no more than 30 per cent of the population can actually attain the preferred marriage.[12] That such demographic factors can place great strains on the marriage rules and modify the stratification system has been argued by Ackerman.[13]

The importance of these marriage selections in the West is attributable to two sources. First, the tendency of family lines to retain relatively similar position in the stratification system over generations is a crucial feature of Western stratification systems. Second, those characteristics that tend to change only at generation intervals, such as race and religion, can introduce constraints upon the distributions of other status symbols that change more frequently. Insofar as it relates to the preservation of restricted marriage markets then segregation in Western societies is also involved.

The substance of this argument is that differential population growth is intimately connected with the systems of stratification and of power in Western nations. Relative position within a nation is significant even if abject poverty no longer exists.

NOTES

1. Simon Kuznets, "Population Change and Aggregate Output," in *Economic Growth and Structure* (New York: Norton, 1965).

2. See Population Division, United Nations, "History of Population Theories" (Note 12, p. 31).

3. Gunnar Myrdal, *Population: A Problem for Democracy* (London: Cambridge U. P., 1940).

4. Georg Simmel, "Quantitative Aspects of the Group," in *The Sociology of Georg Simmel*, trans. and ed. by Kurt H. Wolff (New York: Free Press, 1950), Part I. Parts of this translation are reprinted as "The Significance of Numbers for Social Life," in Paul A. Hare, Edgar F. Borgatta, Robert F. Bates (eds.), *Small Groups: Studies in Social Interaction* (New York: Knopf, 1955).

5. Emile Durkheim, *The Division of Labor in Society*, trans. by G. Simpson (New York: Free Press, 1960).

6. Richard L. Meier, *A Communications Theory of Urban Growth* (Cambridge, Mass.: M.I.T. Press, 1962).

7. John B. Calhoun, "Population Density and Social Pathology," in Leonard J. Duhl (ed.), *The Urban Condition* (New York: Basic Books, 1963).

8. See James M. Beshers, *Urban Social Structure* (New York: Free Press, 1962).

9. Elbridge Sibley, "Some Demographic Clues to Stratification," in Logan Wilson and William L. Kolb (eds.), *Sociological Analysis* (New York: Harcourt, 1949), pp. 642–9.

10. Kingsley Davis and Wilbert E. Moore, "Some Principles of Stratification," in Wilson and Kolb, *op. cit.*, pp. 434–42.

11. David M. Heer, "The Trend of Interfaith Marriages in Canada: 1922–1957," *American Sociological Review*, XXVII, No. 2 (April 1962), 245–50.

12. See: Marion J. Levy, Jr., "A Strategy of Analysis of Variations in Family Structure: Actual Convergence and Ideal Patterns," in American Statistical Association, *Proceedings of the Social Statistics Section* (Washington, D.C., 1964); Ansley J. Coale and Marion J. Levy, Jr. (eds.), *Aspects of the Analysis of Family Structure* (Princeton, N.J.: Princeton U. P., 1965).

13. Charles Ackerman, "Structure and Statistics: The Purum Case," *American Anthropologist*, LXVI, No. 1 (February 1964), 53–64; Charles Ackerman, "Structure and Process: The Purum Case," *American Anthropologist*, LXVII, No. 1 (February 1965), 83–91.

CHAPTER 8

Conclusions

LET us return now to the population crisis in the world today. In the Introduction we inquired into the nature of this crisis, and how we might avert it. What now is our response? What have we learned? Let us step back from the details of technique and fact and seek the more general implications of our knowledge.

The most general implication is this—the population crisis is a social crisis. There are, to be sure, biological aspects, but these have often been exaggerated. We need to understand the dynamics of population growth, the differences between patterns of growth of various nations. These dynamics relate to broader social change. Economics and politics emerge as significant variables in the problem.

To bring out the nature of this social crisis we may examine many nations in turn, each revealing different facets. We must also, however, consider all nations as part of international political and economic systems. The response of each nation to its own internal problems in part depends on its relations with other nations—its place within international systems.

The population crisis, for any given nation, reflects the capacity of that nation to respond to its own social problems. This capacity is like a feedback adjustment; it rests in the national institutions—political, economic, and so on, and in the household decision units as well. Thus the nature of the crisis varies according to the technological capacity of the nation, according to the politically dominant values of the nation, and according to the aspirations of its people. We have used the idea of the demographic transition to bring this out; in particular we have viewed the demographic transition within the larger context of a shift from traditional society to modern society. Roughly, the argument goes that many nations have moved from a situation characterized by low levels of technology, political dominance by a traditional elite opposed to social change, and low aspirations of the people, to a situation characterized by high levels of technology, political dominance by a progressive elite within democratic institutions, and a high level of aspirations. Many other nations show evidence of similar transitions under way. Perhaps such changes will take place even within Communist nations.

Vast demographic changes occur in the process of modernization. The first is the fantastic population growth that occurs, especially when mortality-reducing technology takes effect more rapidly than fertility-reducing technology. It is this change that dominates our fears today. Note that most nations undergoing such rapid population growth are at a relatively low level of technological development, have a relatively low capacity for political adjustment to social change, and have relatively low individual aspirations. The first two points suggest that such a nation has a low capacity to respond to domestic problems. The last point, however, is a storm signal, for if aspirations rise and per capita resources fall then the widening gap could well generate novel political pressures.

In the past, migration could relieve the crisis of growth—migration within countries and migration between countries. Thinly populated frontiers could absorb migrant peoples, and open political borders made this option available to all who could afford transport. Both possibilities have disappeared. Only the urban areas remain open to displaced rural migrants; the capacity of these to absorb new population again turns on economic development and political leadership.

How might the political institutions emerge that would provide progressive leadership? As aspirations and demands increase while technological and political response lags, revolutionary pressures may appear. Fatalism, formerly sanctioned by traditional religion, now may be abandoned; an ideology of activism may emerge. The various Communist revolutions have fed on emerging activism; recently Pope John, Pope Paul, and even the Buddhist monks of Southeast Asia have acknowledged the significance of activist ideology and sought to reorient their religious movements accordingly.

International politics and international economics enter here. For the former implies the rivalries between the Communist nations and the NATO powers while the latter is an essential instrument of this rivalry. It was

Lenin who turned the class system of Marx into a relation between nations, rich and poor. With this instrument international communism could identify the bourgeoisie with imperialism, the imperialism with colonialism and colonialism with the exploitation of the producer of raw materials. In the last twenty years there have been two responses to this challenge, one military and one of aid for economic development. The latter could relieve the population crisis if large-scale introduction of birth control could be appropriately combined with economic development.

Demographic problems can occur even when the transition to modern society is proceeding well. Changing age distributions put new stresses on the economy, especially in the form of services for dependent populations, young and old. Migration and urbanization also produce pressures for new public-service configurations—occupational skills, housing, and transportation must meet new demands.

The resolution of these problems may lie partly in the different traditions or cultures of these nations. It will lie also in the specific mechanism for planning and adjustment—the way in which foresight is built into the political process. A country with a Communist or Socialist tradition may proceed quite differently from one with an ideology of decentralization. The way a country with a cultural tradition disposed to high-density living adjusts to increased urbanization may be different from the adjustment of a country with strong rural cultural themes. (I believe that communism is a late stage of feudalism, one in which the feudal political institutions have been grasped by an elite with an activist and progressive ideology who are nevertheless unable to implement that ideology.)

What is the new relation of the planning process to aspirations of the people? What political means will define this relation? What are the relative roles of progressive elites, of decentralized political power, and of household decision processes in these developments? Is there a new decision-making technology that is relevant to new political institutions? What is the role of the new technocrats of the McNamara revolution? Can they graft the decision-making apparatus of the U.S. Department of Defense onto democratic institutions? Will computers free man or enslave him? These enigmatic questions must receive a mute response.

Our conclusion, then, is that the population problem must be resolved within a broader problem-solving effort. Absorption of increased population must take place within urban areas. This must be done with a comprehensive program—a developing economy and expanding social services. Resources of capital and of management must be marshaled to meet a complex of related social problems; the tactics for resolving demographic aspects must be devised within this larger framework.

APPENDIX

Quantitative Methods[1]

THE quantitative methods in use today in demography have several historical sources. Of these the most important arose in the study of mortality, or deaths. Early public-health leaders assembled mortality records in order to infer cause of disease, especially those causes over which they could assert some influence. In doing so they analyzed deaths by age, sex, and location; perhaps also by occupation or other social characteristics. The basic procedure was to collect records of deaths with the associated characteristics of the persons, and then to cumulate these records until stable differences could be observed in the death rates for one type of person as contrasted with another. In order to calculate a death rate one had to estimate the total number of persons of

(183)

a given type that might have died, the so-called "population at risk," and use this figure as the denominator, with the total number of deaths to persons of that type taken as the numerator. If such denominators could not be obtained directly from data, hypothetical population distributions were constructed that were compatible with the sketchy evidence in hand. These procedures for calculating and comparing death rates were the basic methods of epidemiology.

The study of hypothetical population distributions later became systematized into conventional calculations by actuaries working for insurance companies. The worksheet for these calculations was called a life table. From a given set of death rates specified by age, the actuaries would calculate the implied distribution of lengths of life in the future. Thus they could calculate a price for an insurance premium. Where data failed them, they used theoretical curves. In order to generate future distributions they assumed that a set of death rates was constant with regard to time (but not with regard to age of persons). They summarized the distribution of lengths of life for future age groups by calculating arithmetic means. Of these the mean length of life at birth was the most commonly used statistic.

These early applications illustrate the main principles of subsequent work. The quality and accessibility of data presented major obstacles to any kind of research work; efforts to circumvent these difficulties led to ingenious statistical procedures and to the development of mathematical models. The proper tactics for circumventing the difficulties have depended partly on the quality of the data, but partly also on the purposes of the investigator. These purposes can be divided, for the most part, into the study of deaths in order to explain antecedent causes, and the study of deaths in order to extrapolate future consequences. The former is part of population analysis, the latter part of population projection.

Let us see how the methods for studying deaths carried over to the study of births. The problems of data collection again involve: (1) enumerating births, (2) associating births with other relevant information, e.g., age of mother, and (3) calculating denominators to obtain birth rates from numbers of births.

Births are enumerated directly from continuing record systems, such as vital statistics systems, or estimated indirectly from interviews conducted at a single point in time, such as a census. In the former case one strives for accurate numbers of births—the numerators, while in the latter case one strives for accurate estimates of the total population classified by age and sex—the denominators. Thus in principle both kinds of data are needed. However, one can make crude inferences about denominators from record-keeping systems, and crude inferences about the numerators from census surveys. When both kinds of information are available it is possible to study their consistency and then adjust the data to remove bias. These tasks are best carried out with an explicit mathematical model. Techniques of population projection are often borrowed for consistency tests and for adjusting data before analysis. Thus the procedures for population analysis and population projection are used in combination in research.

Some of the common measures of births need to be defined. With good vital-statistics systems we obtain estimates of the numbers of births. When divided by estimates of the number of women they are called *birth rates*; when divided by estimates of numbers of women by age groups or by marital status they are called *birth rates specified* by age groups or by marital status. With a good census we can estimate the number of children under age 5 as an indicator of recent births; when we divide this estimate by the number of women of childbearing age, say between fifteen and forty-five, then the result is called a *fertility ratio*.

If the ages of mothers are known, either in single years or in five-year age groups, then it is possible to arrange birth rates in successive age groups and to compute the expected distribution of births analogous to the expected lengths of life obtained from age-specific death rates. The mean number of births per mother can then be obtained to summarize this hypothetical distribution of future births (analogous to the mean length of life at birth). This number is called the *gross reproduction rate*.

When adequate information is available on the death rates by age of the female population, the future population of mothers and of children may be adjusted to represent the influence of mortality. The mean number of births per mother for the resulting hypothetical future distribution is the *net reproduction rate*. (The denominator for the mean for both rates is the total number of women entering the childbearing age.)

Suppose we turn our attention to population projection. Frequently one desires to calculate a future population using both birth rates and death rates. The estimates obtained for a closed system (no migration), are often said to be due to "natural increase." Procedures for obtaining such estimates were given explicit mathematical form by A. J. Lotka some forty years ago. He assumed that birth rates and death rates were independent of time but a function of age. Then he deduced the long-term effects on the age structure, namely statistical equilibrium. (His *Elements of Physical Biology*[2] is a classic statement.)

In contemporary terminology we would say that Lotka used the stationary stochastic process as his mathematical model. In particular he studied certain differential equations that arise as hypotheses for the form of the birth and death rates. Thus the problem became one of integration, with the usual approximation formulae, error terms, and so on. (In recent work on epidemiology these methods have been called deterministic due to the form of the differential equation used; Bartlett,[3] Bailey,[4] and others have considered more complicated types of differential equation that are called stochastic.)

Recent extensions of Lotka's work have been made by Coale[5] and Keyfitz.[6] Coale assumes that birth rates are independent of time but death rates change slowly. He obtains an age distribution resembling that derived by Lotka, but which might perhaps be more realistic in application to developing areas.

Keyfitz has extended Lotka's classic work with differential equations to include further characteristics, such as sex and marriage. He has also extended the analogous matrix methods that Lotka recommended late in life. In both instances he has retained the assumption that the rates (or probabilities) are independent of time. Thus the methods are those of the stationary Markov process.

The classic migration statistics have developed along lines similar to those of mortality and fertility. They have, however, been less fully developed because of acute shortages of appropriate data. These shortages stem from the lack of registration statistics on moves from which to compute numerators, as well as a lack of appropriate census measures to compute denominators (the "population at risk").

The former data sources, the continuous registers of population moves by address and person, are especially poorly developed in the United States, in part as they are viewed with suspicion as an aspect of excessive police control. The existence of such registration in Central and Eastern Europe is indeed related to police activities. Such registers in Holland and in Scandinavia, however, exist without conveying these pernicious overtones to the inhabitants.

Even if good registers exist, there is the problem of how to define and tabulate moves. In general, migration is defined with reference to a set of geographical areas. When an address change crosses at least one area boundary it constitutes a case of migration. For a given set of areas and for a given time period one must tabulate moves over all pairs of areas, allowing each to be an origin as well as a destination. The mathematical notation for migration can be either a directed graph or its corresponding matrix defined over all pairs of areas. One's choice of areas can greatly influence the amount and characteristics of migration revealed.

Direct estimates of the appropriate denominators are difficult to obtain from a census. First of all, the census will come at intervals of five to ten years, while registration data would be available on a yearly basis. Even for those years in which the census and registration data match, the census supplies denominators only for the year prior to the move. There are, of course, indirect methods for estimating denominators in the years between censuses, but these methods rely upon linear assumptions that may well be unfounded.

In the United States the best estimates of numerators come from the census. Persons have been asked if they lived in the same house at a previous time and, if the answer were no, they were asked if they had lived in the same city, the same county, or the same state at that time (in 1950 the time was one year previous, in 1940 and 1960 it was five years ago). Either time period precludes using the decennial census to obtain direct estimates of denominators, as the dates fall between censuses.

Methods of estimating denominators and alternative procedures for estimating numerators from U.S. data are described in detail by Shryock.[7]

We should underline the significance of denominators in classic demographic analysis. The denominators were needed to make comparisons. More than that, the successive selection of different denominators was the crucial step in analysis. The successive selection of denominators tended toward greater specificity in the "population at risk," thus allowing new variables to enter into the comparisons of rates. But the inclusion of more variables was only sanctioned after the analytic consequences of a previous reduced set had been determined. For example, birth rates were computed for the female population, then for specified ages of the female population, then for marital status, residence and so on.

In effect the theory of a demographer was revealed in his selection of denominators. In particular he could choose his denominators in order to eliminate the influence of some variables so the influence of other variables could be more clearly revealed in the comparison of rates. Thus, for example, the influence of age and sex distributions upon births could be removed (or at least greatly reduced) in order that the influence of marital status or of occupation might be more clearly examined.

These tasks were never easy. Any set of denominators was difficult to estimate. Many alternative denominators could be conceptually defined; the choice for estimation was not simplified by this variety. In particular the research necessary to obtain one estimate might yield little information about another. Compounding these difficulties was the fact that the estimates of denominators were not always independent of the estimates of the numerators. If a number of births in a given year were divided by the average total population during that year, the births might appear in both numerator and denominator. (For this reason it is best to divide by the population at the beginning of the year—as suggested by the mathematics of conditional probability.)

Let us now develop an argument for a different set of mathematical models and associated statistical concepts from the classic methods described above. There are three points of difference we wish to emphasize: (1) The probabilities are assumed to be nonstationary, i.e., they may change over time. (2) These probabilities are in part a function of social change, the diffusion of new technology and new social variables throughout a social system, perhaps viewed as an outcome of a social psychological decision process in the household constrained by larger social processes. (3) These probabilities can be represented in a "cohort" model—each person is characterized by his own age and date of birth, and separate probabilities of birth are defined for these characteristics.

When we assume that the probabilities do not change we have access to a well-established body of mathematical theorems that define the state of the system in the short run and the long run (in transient and in equilibrium states). But if we drop this assumption, and allow the probabilities to change, we cannot use these theorems. Therefore we must adopt another set of tactics in order to describe the behavior of the system. So long as the change in probabilities is defined by an explicit rule, the computations can be carried out with a digital computer. This is not a simple matter; programming the computer as one task and selecting reasonable rules for changing probabilities as another, can lead to great difficulties.

The most straightforward assumption of changing probabilities is a simple curve, linear or exponential, estimated from previous experience. In mortality, for example, one can take present rates for a non-Western country and extrapolate them on a curve that will be asymptotic to present rates for a Western country in forty years, or some other time lag; this is the approach taken by Brackett.[8]

We shall, however, take a more complex approach. Our explicit rule for changing probabilities will be derived from the other two points of emphasis, social change and cohort aspects.

Let us show how these three have worked together in the past. Cohort techniques have been used in mortality and in migration, but they are best known for their use by P. K. Whelpton in the analysis and projection of births.[9] We shall indicate their use in mortality statistics for definitional simplicity, then turn our attention to births for elaboration.

The cohort is a set of persons born in the same time period. They are then traced as they age and their experience is recorded. Thus the cohort death rates and cohort birth rates represent the experience of these persons as they age. These cohort rates are not the same as the age-specific rates calculated from the experience recorded within one calendar year, the so-called period rates. In particular, social change will be reflected differently by the cohort rates than by the period rates. We use this fact for both research purposes mentioned previously, analysis of past rates and projection of future rates.

A classic example of the analysis of cohort mortality rates is provided by Merrell.[10] She provides a table of age-specific mortality rates from tuberculosis for Massachusetts males. The rows of the table are ages with ten-year intervals, while the columns of the table are dates with ten-year intervals. The period age specific rates are contained in any column, but the cohort age-specific rates are diagonals, say age 10 in 1890, age 20 in 1900, age 30 in 1910, and so on. The period rates are summarized in one chart, the cohort rates in another; they lead to very different interpretations of the historical trend in mortality from tuberculosis. From the period perspective the effect of social change (medical technology) is to shift the age at which tuberculosis strikes, but from the cohort perspective the effect is to reduce mortality at all ages but to retain the same age distribution.

Table A-1 — Age-specific death rates per 100,000 from tuberculosis for Massachusetts males, 1880 to 1940, with rates for cohort of 1880 indicated

Age	1880	1890	1900	1910	1920	1930	1940
0– 4	760	578	309	209	108	41	11
5– 9	43	49	31	21	24	11	2
10–19	126	115	90	63	49	21	4
20–29	444	361	288	207	149	81	35
30–39	378	368	296	253	164	115	51
40–49	364	336	253	253	175	118	86
50–59	366	325	267	252	171	127	92
60–69	475	346	304	246	172	95	109
70 +	672	396	343	163	127	95	79

* Margaret Merrell, "Time-Specific Life Tables and Observed Survivorship," in Joseph J. Spengler and Otis Dudley Duncan (eds.), *Demographic Analysis* (New York: Free Press, 1956), p. 113.

The most extensive use of cohort concepts is due to P. K. Whelpton. He used them to obtain a historical series of estimates of probabilities of birth by date of birth, by age and by number of previous children; he then analyzed these historical data. He also developed cohort notions for population projection.

Figure A–1

Age-Specific Death Rates from Tuberculosis for Different Calendar Years, Massachusetts Males

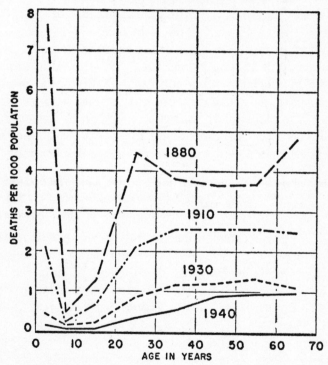

Source: Margaret Merrell, "Time-Specific Life Tables and Observed Survivorship," in Joseph J. Spengler and Otis Dudley Duncan (eds.), *Demographic Analysis* (New York: Free Press, 1956), p. 112.

Figure A–2

Age-Specific Death Rates from Tuberculosis for Successive 10-year Cohorts, Massachusetts Males

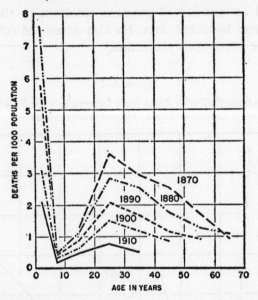

Source: Margaret Merrell, "Time-Specific Life Tables and Observed Survivorship" in Joseph J. Spengler and Otis Dudley Duncan (eds.) *Demographic Analysis* (New York: Free Press, 1956), p. 114.

Whelpton's contribution to analysis was a monumental reconstruction of historical time series from vital-statistics records. He derived estimates of numbers of births to women of a given age, given date of birth, and given number of previous children for each year since 1917. Ages and dates of birth are given in single years. Numbers of previous children are in eight categories from 0, 1, to 7-and-up. The series is available for all women, and for native white women. He also estimates appropriate denominators. Thus the probability of a birth in a given year to a woman of a specified age, birth date, and number of previous children can be calculated from these data. In fact the whole set of probabilities for all women and for native white women has been calculated.

Much more research can be done now with these data with the advent of digital computers. But Whelpton was able to increase our understanding of U.S. birth patterns greatly by intelligent inspection of the data. The drastic drop in annual births in the 1930's could be related to new patterns of family formation. The data suggested a great increase in the amount of effective family planning; Whelpton called it a postponement of births in reaction to the economic crisis. The "baby boom" of the late 1940's and early 1950's was initially composed of first and second births, especially to young people. Whelpton, and most other demographers, thought the effect would level off, or even temporarily diminish, for the higher-order births if the new families were to achieve the average family size of the 1930's. Instead the new families adopted new patterns of family formation. The very large and very small families both became more rare, with three, four, or five children becoming the typical size. Interestingly enough, the women who began family formation in the 1930's did not make up their postponements after the war; it seemed as if a completely new style of family formation had begun in a new generation.

Many people noted that Whelpton did not always guess right as to the future style of family formation. One should also observe, however, that without his analysis of the data it would have been difficult to make any guess at all, and even more difficult to determine which guess was sustained by the data. If our only indicator of changing birth patterns was the annual volume of births we would have difficulty inferring the effects upon patterns of family formation, save in ten-year intervals from the decennial census results.

Whelpton paralleled his analysis of vital statistics with studies aimed at elucidating changing practices and attitudes that might suggest future styles of family formation. He was a senior staff member of the Indianapolis study of the 1930's and early 1940's, and collaborated with the Survey Research Center at the University of Michigan in the late 1950's and early 1960's in further studies of this type.[11]

These experiences greatly influenced Whelpton's approach to the projection of future births. At first he simply extrapolated the previous family-formation styles, and in consequence underestimated the extent and magnitude of the baby boom. After this experience, however, he assigned less importance to the extrapolation of past birth probabilities in projecting future births. He turned his efforts toward more precise measurement and understanding of family-size ideals and preferences. This tack led him to stress the intentions of younger people as a basis for extrapolating their subsequent behavior.

We also wish to extrapolate future births from a social psychological perspective, but we want to include two phenomena explicitly—the diffusion of planning and the sensitivity of planners to changes in economic and social conditions. Thus we follow Whelpton in assuming that the birth probabilities change and that cohort methods are appropriate in the study of past changes as well as the extrapolation of future changes. We differ in our more elaborate attempt to represent social change explicitly in our models. The difference stems in part from our desire to extend the method to areas of high fertility in which traditional society is being permeated by new technology and attitudes. Further, however, we desire a better understanding of the way in which the social psychology of the family reflects larger social change. This latter desire does not stem from a belief that we can readily project social change into the future, but from an intent to adjust our birth projections should social change occur.

The statistical and mathematical implications of my argument have been set forth in two articles[12] and are being implemented in my present program of computer research. Assume that the population consists of nonplanners and of planners. The argument is that, within a cohort model, the birth probabilities can be expressed as a function of (1) a diffusion parameter that determines the rate at which nonplanners are converted to planners, and (2) an explicit decision model for the behavior of the planners. The arithmetic can be compactly represented in matrix algebra; computer representation is also straightforward. The population projections that are calculated may be summarized by various statistics. In particular the annual births in any one year and the cumulative births of any cohort up to any given age are provided by the program that we use.

The calculations are so convenient and inexpensive that one can carry out a number of them based on different assumptions, and then compare the results. In this situation an entirely new possibility arises, that of comparing the effects of different population policies. This useful task is currently being implemented in our program of research.

The situation in migration has some parallels, but an important difference. The parallels lie in the three points that characterize our approach-changing probabilities, decision theory, and cohort models. The difference is that there has been no Whelpton to assemble data that permits estimation of transition probabilities.

Using the parallels I have constructed computer models of cohort migration. My problem now is to obtain reasonable constraints on the transition probabilities. These constraints stem partly from fugitive information on the relative magnitudes of the probabilities and partly from the study of the implications of the probabilities— the kinds of projections that result.

In order to indicate the character of these cohort computer models I shall present the mathematical notation. The fertility model assumes a particularly simple form. The notation presented here has a set of birth probabilities as essential parameters. There are two considerations in the definition of the parameters: (1) Given these parameters, the following measures of fertility can be deduced—cumulative birth distributions at any age (a census concept), average size of completed family (a census concept), annual births (a vital statistics concept), and spacing of births (a census concept). (2) The estimation of these parameters is made feasible by the empirical time series constructed by the late P. K. Whelpton.[13]

For any given cohort (women born in a given year) we wish to produce the annual distribution of women by number of children, the cumulative births to a given age, and the annual births at each age. We will choose our definitions to be consistent with the form of Whelpton's empirical probabilities.

The probabilities are defined over eight categories: 0 children, 1 child, 2 children, and so on, to 7-and-up children. Each woman is allowed to have only one child in one year. Thus, having a birth in a year is equivalent to moving to the next category for all categories except the last.

A matrix of such probabilities is defined for each cohort and each age. Let age $= x$, cohort $= T$, then the matrix

$$
Px^T = 1 \quad
\begin{array}{c}
\\
0 \\
\\
\\
\\
\\
\\
7 \text{ and up}
\end{array}
\overset{\displaystyle 0 \quad\; 1 \qquad\cdots\qquad\quad 7\text{ up}}{
\left[
\begin{array}{cccccc}
P_{11} & P_{12} & 0 & \cdots & & 0 \\
0 & P_{22} & P_{23} & 0 & \cdots & 0 \\
0 & 0 & P_{33} & P_{34} & \cdots & 0 \\
\cdot & \cdot & \cdot & \cdot & & \\
\cdot & \cdot & \cdot & \cdot & & \\
\cdot & \cdot & \cdot & \cdot & & \\
0 & 0 & 0 & 0 & \cdots & 1
\end{array}
\right]}
$$

contains only two nonzero entries in each row, save for the last row, which contains only a 1 in the diagonal. (A special adjustment must be made for births to the 7-and-up category.)

Let us describe a single cohort and thus dispense with the superscript T. Within this cohort we will define all births as occurring to women of ages 14–49, inclusively.

The distribution of women at any given age is defined by a vector: $M_x = (M_{x1}, M_{x2}, \cdots, M_{x8})$, where M_{x1} is the number of women at age x with 0 children, and so on, up to M_{x8}, which is the number of women at age x with 7-and-up children.

We may define the computation of M_{x+1} from M_x and P_x (the previous age) by starting at age 14 and proceeding through all ages. If we subtract 13 from x, the equations are $M_1 P_1 = M_2$; $M_2 P_2 = M_3$; and so on for all ages. By substituting for M_2 in the second equation its value in the first equation, we have $M_1 P_1 P_2 = M_3$. In general, we have the product of the initial M vector and successive P matrices:

$$M_1 \prod_{i=1}^{k} P_i = M_{k+1}$$

From these cumulative distributions we obtain cumulative births by multiplying the number of persons in each category by the number of children associated with that category, save for the 7-and-up category which requires a special procedure. Annual births are obtained by computing differences between successive cumulative births.

Migration cohort models incorporate different parameters according to the set of areas defined; thus migration between metropolitan areas reflects the working of job markets whereas migration within metropolitan areas reflects housing markets (in particular rent, social status and life cycle characteristics of housing).

The migration cohort models, however, must depart from the assumptions of the fertility models. In particular the saturation effects of population in attractive areas can be included if we total the population across age groups in each area in each year. Thus we cannot calculate the time path of each cohort independently of the time paths of the other cohorts which must compete for the same jobs and housing. We must represent this queuing effect, which has some analogies to the college admissions problem, but with quotas less fixed—for example, the housing market can more readily expand in response to demand.

These models are only part of a larger interest in social systems. Currently I am developing a cohort demographic model that will include birth, death, migration and social mobility as components into which the above notions will be incorporated. The interested reader should consult "Birth Projections with Cohort Models," *Demography*, vol. II (1965); "Fertility Models with Social Parameters," *Proceedings of the Social Statistics Section*, 1964 Annual Meeting of the American Statistical Association; "Substantive Issues in Models of Large Scale Social Systems," *Computer Methods in the Analysis of Large Scale Social Systems*; and "Social Status and Social Change" (with Stanley Reiter), *Behavioral Science* (January 1963).

NOTES

1. Another helpful treatment is Leo Silberman, "Essential Statistical Concepts and Models in Demography," in Paul H. Landis, *Population Problems*, 2d ed. prepared by Paul K. Hatt (New York: American Book, 1954).

2. Republished as *Elements of Mathematical Biology* (New York: Dover, 1956).

3. Maurice S. Bartlett, *Stochastic Population Models in Ecology and Epidemiology* (New York: Wiley, 1960).

4. Norman T. J. Bailey, *The Elements of Stochastic Processes with Applications to the Natural Sciences* (New York: Wiley, 1964).

5. Ansley J. Coale, "Estimates of Various Demographic Measures Through the Quasi-Stable Age Distribution," in *Emerging Techniques in Population Research* (New York: Milbank Memorial Fund, 1962), pp. 175–93.

6. Nathan Keyfitz, "Matrix Multiplication as a Technique of Population Analysis," *Milbank Memorial Fund Quarterly*, XLII, No. 4, Part 1 (October 1964), 68–84; Nathan Keyfitz, "The Population Projection as a Matrix Operator," *Demography*, I, No. 1 (1964), 56–73; Nathan Keyfitz and Edmund M. Murphy, "How Much Demographic Return Can a Single Program Extract?" in James M. Beshers (ed.), *Computer Methods in the Analysis of Large Scale Social Systems* (Cambridge, Mass.: Joint Center for Urban Studies, 1965), pp. 53–9.

7. See Note 7, page 150.

8. James W. Brackett, "Some Computer Applications to Population Projections and Demographic Analysis," in James M. Beshers (ed.), *op. cit.*, pp. 60–67.

9. An excellent summary of Whelpton's approach can be found in Wilson H. Grabill, Clyde V. Kiser, and Pascal K. Whelpton, *The Fertility of American Women* (New York: Wiley, 1958), Chap. 9.

10. Margaret Merrell, "Time-Specific Life Tables Contrasted with Observed Surviorship," in Joseph J. Spengler and Otis Dudley Duncan (eds.), *Demographic Analysis* (New York: Free Press, 1956), pp. 108–14.

11. See Note 1, p. 128 and Note 12, p. 129.

12. James M. Beshers, "Birth Projections with Cohort Models," *Demography*, II (1965), 593–9; "Substantive Issues in Models of Large-Scale Social Systems," in Beshers (ed.), *op. cit.*, pp. 85–91.

13. Especially the unpublished birth probabilities at the National Vital Statistics Division.

Index